Word from My Kings and Queens
Overcoming Seemingly Insurmountable Odds

A collection of triumphant stories compiled by

Marvin "Merv" Mattair

Word from My Kings & Queens
Compilation copyright © 2011 by Marvin T. Mattair

All rights reserved. No part of this book may be reproduced in any form without the express written permission of the publisher or individual authors.

Published by:
Amani Publishing, LLC
P. O. Box 12045
Tallahassee, FL 32317
www.AmaniPublishing.net
850.264.3341

A company based on faith, hope, and love

ISBN-13: 9780981584782

LCCN: 2011902497

Cover photograph courtesy of: **Istockphoto.com**

This book is a work of nonfiction. Some of the names may have been changed to protect privacy. However, the authors have made a good faith effort to render the truth or essence of events the way they remember them.

DEDICATION

This book is dedicated to a male nurse by the name of Mr. HB, who worked for the Madison County Memorial Hospital, in Madison, Florida. Mr. HB's actions saved the physical structure of my family on September 11, 2008. I am immensely grateful and honored to give this recognition to him because he not only saved the life of my little son, but he fortified a fact about life. Mr. HB, a white male, saved the life of a fragile, premature African-American boy.

Black and white played no role in this "life and death" dilemma. He simply saw a baby that was slipping into another realm and took care of an urgent and apparent need. A miracle occurred! Our son, TJ, breathed life, and Mr. HB shed tears of thanksgiving.

Mr. HB confirmed the fact that we should not take someone else's emergency for granted or look down on anyone because of their skin color, social status, economic status, gender, age, or personal struggles. We never know what the next minute has in store for our lives or the person who will have to *reach out, and pull us out of a life or death situation.*

Rest in peace, Mr. HB, because before you lost your life in 2010, you saved our precious son, TJ, and we are tremendously grateful. Please read the extended dedication to Mr. HB in the story titled, *You Saved Me.*

TABLE OF CONTENTS

1. My Personal Bully (Alan Anderson) 7
2. From Bully to Brother (David Jonas) 12
3. Not Another Statistic (Denise Robinson) 16
4. Right Road, Wrong Time (Kelvin E. Mattair) 20
5. A Female Athlete Dealing with Disappointment (Tameika Ashley Jonas) 24
6. Believe in His Plan (Craig Wilson) 29
7. Journey to a Conquering, Overcoming & Triumphant Spirit (Edna Haynes-Turner) 34
8. That Can Never Happen to Me (Marvin "Merv" Mattair) 39
9. The Amazing Journey of Healing (Angela Y. Hodge) 45
10. Saved for Greatness (Gerald Bullocks) 48
11. Personal Struggles of a Fatherless Girl (Meshalene Love-Taylor) 53
12. Chasing a Dream (Marcus Hawkins) 57
13. From Poverty to the President's Office (Leslie DeRenzo) 62
14. Stepping into Greatness (Gerald P. Simmons, Jr.) 66
15. Overcoming the Struggles of a Child with Chronic Illness (Dawn Desiree Banks) 70
16. Real Life (Brian Sanderson) 74
17. Be a Survivor, I Am (Roshanda Denson) 81
18. A Quest for Manhood (David Dukes) 88
19. From Stuttering to Motivational Speaking (Marvin "Merv" Mattair) 93

INTRODUCTION

Previously, we have given you, *Word to My Kings & Queens: Achieving a Renewed & Improved Mind,* and now it's time for you to hear, *Word from My Kings & Queens: Overcoming Seemingly Insurmountable Odds.* This book is a collection of triumphant stories from normal, everyday, hardworking people who were faced with challenges and adversities in their lives. Challenges and adversities that seemed or deemed insurmountable, and without a solution, but they triumphantly overcame. They have chosen to share their stories for the apparent purpose of being the *hope giver* in the lives of individuals who no longer have an anchor. Their stories are shared so that others are able to recapture the hope that has been lost. They were shared to prayerfully provide guidance to those who have lost their direction, or don't have clarity for their journey.

The authors have shared to provide motivation for persons who are not inspired or lack enthusiasm for life. Destiny cannot be accomplished when one is not experiencing peace, and some of the stories leave the message that peace is attainable. These authors have stepped out on faith to hopefully empower the readers mentally, emotionally, and spiritually. Lives can be saved and destinies changed, therefore, no longer can we take stories of this magnitude to our graves. *When we become strengthened, we are to strengthen others.*

You are about to read stories from Kings & Queens of different races and genders, so prepare your minds and hearts to go on this triumphant journey from the first story to the very last one.

INTENTIONS

Our intentions are for you to know that there are no obstacles in your life, if you are at least trying, that you can't overcome. Being a king or queen is not about possessing lots of jewelry, crowns, and being a part of a lineage of earthly royalty. Rather it can be identified and defined as having a lot of self control, self respect, morals, standards, love, and living in royalty knowing that you are in control of your own thoughts and actions.

We expect you to learn from the challenges and mistakes of each author and refuse to allow yourself to go through the same things that they experienced. It is important that we stop repeating the same, preventable mistakes. These stories can help to facilitate this process by applying the wisdom of these authors. The stories you are about to read are taken from the fabric of real life individuals and not from the pages of a fairytale. So, be cognizant of the fact that the outcomes of their struggles may differ from yours. However, the outcomes are triumphant ones. Our intention is that you mentally enter into this literature and exit with a renewed mind because, "YOU ARE ROYALTY."

1
MY PERSONAL BULLY
Alan Anderson

What began as some of the most frightening days of my childhood can now be remembered and revered as the very things that have made me who I am today. I am not sure if thankful can be used as a word that defines how I feel about my experience, but for now, it is the closest word that I can find to describe the culmination of my journey. I was bullied and tormented with laughter and ridicule and at the time, I truly thought that I would have to endure that for my entire life. I thought this was normal and that everyone had a personal bully.

I met him when I was in elementary school. This seemingly nice boy from the neighborhood became *my personal bully* overnight. David was known as one of the poor kids in the school and initially, I thought that he was my friend. To befriend him, I gave him money and food from my lunch, and he seemed appreciative. In return, he talked to me, and I got to play with cool kids that had never spoken to me before. It was a reasonable price to pay for being accepted.

When the bullying began, I would avoid him, but he would seek me out to get my money. I began telling my mother that I might be too sick to go to school, but eventually, she caught on that my sicknesses were made up. I was made to go to school and face the music. Some days were calm, and David would find someone else to pick on or would not seem overly interested in picking on me. Other days, he would come after me with a vengeance that started making me believe that I had done something to deserve this treatment.

At a young age, I quickly found out the meaning of "taking kindness as a weakness." In my case, my weakness was indeed my kindness. David learned the same lesson. When I decided to not share my money or when the lunch was too good to cut in half, David found a way to get it anyway. My good days at school were when David did not come to school or when I could stay close to my teacher who became my safe zone. David gained confidence and notoriety as his audience of laughing students increased.

Going to school became increasingly difficult for me and my parents could not understand why I hated school. My mother also could not understand why I came home from school hungry every day. I am sure that she questioned why the school was not feeding her son well. She never asked, and I never told her that *my personal bully* came calling when he wanted money.

I tried ignoring him which only made him angrier. For the most part, I would zone out on the name calling and for the not so idle threats, I tried threatening back with, "I'm telling the teacher." When I did, David warned that he would get me after school. For me, his warnings were kept in high regard. My walks home became a frantic dash for my house or hiding in the bushes until the coast was clear. The green hedges that lined the streets on the way home became a refuge. This made me internalize as I created my own world, a world where everyone loved me. I was popular and admired like a hero. I found myself alone most of the time, and I lacked confidence in myself and trust in the world around me.

My source of love was my family, my church, and the different people who led with good examples on how to overcome obstacles. This close group saw the good in me, and they expected my best with anything I did, and I was going to prove them right. One elder told me, "Fear is just a part of life, and if you keep moving forward, you can achieve anything you desire." My mother said, "When you fall, you get back up, dust yourself off, and continue doing what you were doing. If you don't get back up, you give up on yourself." Those were words that stuck with me.

My personal bully had a much more profound effect on me, but everything began to make sense when one day I saw David in a totally different light. After our normal routine of him taking my money, this kid was doing the very same thing to David that he had been doing to me. He was bullying David out of the money he had taken from me. *My personal bully* had his own "personal bully."

He was vulnerable and in a twisted way, I found myself happy that it was not me and sad for him. I was in search of acceptance which made me an easy target, but maybe David was too.

David continued bullying me for quite some time. I don't remember where I got the strength from, but one day it came to an end. I looked into David's eyes and told him, "You don't scare me anymore. I don't owe you anything, no money, no food, and I don't need you as a friend because I have friends." From that day on, I never looked back. David was a part of my past, or so I thought.

He came back into my life in 1992. I was living in Tampa, Florida, and so did David. Now our friendship is based on love and respect for each other. David was all grown up, and we were given the opportunity to reestablish something that we originally had when we started this brotherhood in elementary school. He seemed at ease with rebuilding our friendship, but I had to go inside in order to search myself and let go of all the pain I had experienced as a child. I had to learn to trust him. Our friendship continues to grow, and I no longer dwell in the past. I look forward to our friendship as we become grandparents and great grandparents and share life stories with the ones we love. I hope that our past helps someone in the future.

Bullying is never easy to resolve, but often times, a bully gains momentum based on how you react to being bullied. The more you react with fear, the more they will feel that they can treat you like the victim that you have become. You can get them to stop.

Here are some tips to try if you, or someone you know, find themselves at the mercy of a bully:

1. The most important thing to do is to tell someone. It would be better to tell a teacher or a parent, but you can also tell a friend. If telling someone does not work the first time, go to another teacher or another parent or another friend and keep telling, until someone takes action. Make sure to write down the dates, times, places, and witnesses that observe the bullying.

2. Try to ignore the bully and walk away. It would be very hard for a bully to continue bullying, if there is no one there to bully. Don't be afraid of people seeing you leave. It is not worth getting hurt to keep money or possessions. Possessions can be replaced.

3. If possible, try not to show how scared or upset you are. If you show that you don't care, they may lose interest. Say "No" firmly and turn away calmly. You can practice this in a mirror.

4. Try to avoid being alone in places where you know the bully is likely to pick on you. Surrounding yourself with friends is a good deterrent.

Fighting is never the answer, however, if you are in a situation where you must act, only do so to defend yourself from bodily harm and only with the same or equal means that your attacker is using. Example, if a bully continues to push you, you push back. You can't take up a baseball bat and use it against a push.

Alan Anderson
Email: alanandersond@yahoo.com

MY THOUGHTS

How did this story impact you mentally?

_____
_____
_____
_____

These are the people that I will talk to if I am faced with what this author was faced with:

_____
_____
_____
_____

These are the people that I need to reach out to that may be struggling with what this author struggled with but don't have a clue that they can overcome it:

_____
_____
_____
_____

Self Motivation

I _____ understand that knowledge itself holds no power, until it is applied to our lives through our actions. I can overcome this seemingly insurmountable odd because I am Royalty from birth, making me ruler over my decisions. I will no longer live my life doubting what I am capable of overcoming.

YOU CAN CHANGE A LIFE AS WELL BY SHARING YOUR STORY........ROYALTY@MYEXCEL.COM

2
FROM BULLY TO BROTHER
David Jonas

My name is David Jonas. I want to share a part of my life that I am not so proud of, and I also hope that it can help someone in the process. During my younger years at Madison Middle School, I was guilty of bullying a young boy name Alan. I make no excuses for what I did because at the time, I was a very selfish young boy. I was born in Madison, Florida, to a single mom with eleven siblings, and we had much love in our family. We were a poor family that didn't have much to our name, but we continued to trust one another and have faith in God.

At that point in my life, I knew that I could get whatever I wanted by force. I had known Alan for the majority of my life and we had a pretty good relationship until elementary school. When I saw Alan, I saw a friend, but also a person who I could take advantage of. We grew up in the same neighborhood, but we had very different lifestyles. When I looked at Alan's lifestyle as a young boy, I was very envious because I knew he had more than I could ever have. I can remember going to school very hungry, looking for a way to get money. I knew that Alan was my friend so he would "spot me a few dollars." This continued to go on for some weeks until it turned into the bullying phase.

I began talking mean to Alan and doing anything to intimidate him to get what I wanted. I would threaten him and say, "If I don't get your money I will beat you up."

Even though I intimidated him, I never fought him. I would come to school, talk down to him, and make him feel miserable. I would find him at the cafeteria, daunt him, and take his lunch. Like any other day, I was looking for Alan to give me what I wanted at the time. When we would meet up, I continued my regular routine behavior of bullying him, but this time was different. This type of behavior existed for a long time and continued to progress, causing me to lose a friendship. Alan stood up to me!

He realized that what I was doing was wrong, and he wasn't going to take it anymore. Alan made the decision to walk away from this situation; I gained so much respect for him that the bullying came to an end.

Immediately after getting out of the military, my family decided that we would reside in Tampa, Florida. One day during my regular routines, I ended up running into Alan. It had been many years since we had seen each other; so the moment was very surreal. We exchanged numbers and started to communicate. Even though we never had the best relationship, it was important for me to show him how much I was concerned. During the process of learning each other, we built a bond that required us to trust and look out for one another. I wanted him to forgive me for what I had done, but I didn't know how to ask. So I took it upon myself to show him how much his friendship meant to me. My actions allowed Alan to experience trust in me again and become secure in knowing that I would never try to take advantage of him again. Being a Christian man, I always knew that God puts people in your life for a reason, and at that time in Alan's life, I was there when he needed me the most. I took honor and pride in being Alan's friend. I will never let anything come between the <u>bond</u> we have for one another.

I can recall, as a young man, asking God for forgiveness and giving me the opportunity to undo all the wrong I had done to our friendship. I knew at the time of my bullying that I was wrong, but I didn't want to stop. I didn't realize that I was losing someone that really was a true friend. I was always ashamed of what I did to Alan. As an African-American man, I realize that people take advantage of my kindness as well. So I always make it a point to talk about how you should treat people. Getting the opportunity to change a negative situation to a positive was something I was grateful for. I was never proud of how I acted towards Alan and our friendship. I needed him to understand that I wanted his true forgiveness.

Since the time we ran into each other, our friendship has grown more and more each day. We are more like brothers than friends. During my childhood, I did things I was not proud of to Alan, and I was given the second chance to make things right. You never know how much you can affect someone else's life because of something that you may do or say to them. As I was growing up, and I'm pretty sure you heard the saying also, "If you have nothing nice to say, don't say anything at all."

One thing that I want you to always remember: Words are the most powerful things in the world; they can either make or break you. Even if a situation seems right to you, and you have no problem with it (for example my bullying Alan), you never know how that other person is feeling or how adversely they are affected. Just always remember, and ask yourself, "What if that was me in their shoes?"

David Jonas
Email: 1234jonas@msn.com

MY THOUGHTS

How did this story impact you mentally?
_____
_____
_____
_____

These are the people that I will talk to if I am faced with what this author was faced with:
_____
_____
_____
_____

These are the people that I need to reach out to that may be struggling with what this author struggled with but don't have a clue that they can overcome it:
_____
_____
_____
_____

Self Motivation

I _____ understand that knowledge itself holds no power, until it is applied to our lives through our actions. I can overcome this seemingly insurmountable odd because I am Royalty from birth, making me ruler over my decisions. I will no longer live my life doubting what I am capable of overcoming.

3
NOT ANOTHER STATISTIC
Denise Robinson

As a young girl, I took pride in doing my best educationally. My mother was an educator, and my father was in the Army. I enjoyed making good grades and loved school until my dad was sent to Korea, and we decided to move back to my parents' home town of Madison, Florida. I had never lived in a rural community and experienced cultural shock when we arrived. We moved to Madison County when I entered into the sixth grade. Even though the majority of my family lived in Madison, I felt like an outsider. I had few friends, and even some of my cousins did not want to hang with me.

I was confused because every school I attended, it was always easy for me to make friends, but it did not happen in Madison. I soon found out that people did not like the way I talked because it was considered "talking white." So I did what most children do and that was to conform to what my peers expected me to act like. I continued to pride myself in making good grades, but I began to allow my standards to be lowered, instead of staying true to myself. This continued into high school, and I found myself trying to really fit in with my peers.

During conversations with the "clique" that I hung with in high school, everyone in the group was sexually active except me. They would discuss in details what they did, what it was like, and everyone had a story, except me. So what did I do? Well, I decided to have sex with my boyfriend in order to have "a story of my own" to tell. Guess what? I was the one, and the only one in my "clique" to get pregnant. I became pregnant at the age of fifteen, and I was in the eleventh grade. My life completely changed when I found out I was pregnant. The same group of friends began talking about me as though I was some kind of slut. They were doing the same thing I had done, but they did not get pregnant. Remember, when I said I prided myself in getting good grades, well once it was known that, "Denise was pregnant," I was immediately treated differently.

My father wanted to throw me out, my mother was extremely disappointed and wouldn't talk to me. My church family shunned me away and made me feel less than a person. My teachers treated me differently, and I even overheard one saying, "I thought she was smart." I felt lower than dirt, and all I wanted to do was to get rid of this baby that was inside of me. I tried so many different ways that I had heard that would get rid of a baby. I tried drinking vinegar, picking up my bed and other heavy objects that I thought would cause me to have a miscarriage, but nothing worked. I even had a conversation with my parents about having an abortion, but they were not having it. My mother informed me emphatically, that I was having my baby and finishing school.

As the pregnancy became more obvious, I got more depressed about being pregnant. I heard comments like: I was going to be another black teenage mother that is going to be on welfare. One day at school, my Spanish teacher, Mrs. James, pulled me to the side to talk to me. She looked me in the eyes and told me, "Stop having a pity party for yourself." I remember that conversation as though it was yesterday. She told me that I was not the first and will not be the last teenager to get pregnant. She told me not to let anyone tell me that I'm not smart or make me feel as though they are perfect because no one is perfect. She informed me that many of my teachers have skeletons in their closets, and have no right looking down on me.

Mrs. James told me to hold my head up high and continue to strive, and one stumbling block does not keep you down; it may slow you down, but don't let it ever stop you. At that moment, I was determined not to be *another statistic*. I was going to complete high school, and I was going to finish college.

I had my son on March 13, 1997. I had enough credits and the grade point average to graduate from Madison County High School my junior year at the age of sixteen. I enrolled at North Florida Community College in August and worked at Winn-Dixie for two years. I graduated from North Florida Community College with an Associate of Arts degree at the age of eighteen and transferred to Valdosta State University. I continued working and commuted to VSU. While I was attending VSU, I became depressed again because of having a child. I was attending a major university but could not attend any of the festivities.

My parents were adamant in saying, "Where you go, your son goes." The only time she watched my son was when I was working. I wasn't able to attend homecomings, parties, go to the clubs or other festivities like I wanted to. Several times I wanted to quit school and work full time. I wanted to have money to buy a car, or like some of my friends, have the ability to be able to get my own apartment so that I could move out of my parents' home.

Not long after I started feeling sorry for myself, my cousin, Alisha Davis was killed in a car accident on her way home from work. I was devastated and did not understand why she was the one who had to die. Alisha was a good girl compared to me, and I did not understand why; but I realized after her death that God had me on this earth for a reason. After her death, I stopped feeling sorry for myself and was determined to finish school and fulfill my goals. I continued to attend Valdosta State University and graduated, May 2001, with my Bachelor in Sociology at the age of twenty.

I am now thirty-years-old, married to a wonderful God-fearing man, Tharron Robinson, and we have three beautiful children: Deonte (13), Zarrion (7), and A'Nesha (5). I also just graduated with my Master in Sociology, in May 2010, from Valdosta State University; and I am currently enrolled in school to obtain a Ph.D. in Human Services. I enjoy empowering other young mothers to pursue their goals and dreams, no matter their situation. Being a teenage mother does not make you *another statistic*; with God, you can achieve whatever you set your mind to, combined with perseverance and hard work.

Denise Robinson
Email: denise.robinson30@gmail.com

MY THOUGHTS

How did this story impact you mentally?
_____
_____
_____
_____

These are the people that I will talk to if I am faced with what this author was faced with:
_____
_____
_____
_____

These are the people that I need to reach out to that may be struggling with what this author struggled with but don't have a clue that they can overcome it:
_____
_____
_____
_____

Self Motivation

I _____ understand that knowledge itself holds no power, until it is applied to our lives through our actions. I can overcome this seemingly insurmountable odd because I am Royalty from birth, making me ruler over my decisions. I will no longer live my life doubting what I am capable of overcoming.

YOU CAN CHANGE A LIFE AS WELL BY SHARING YOUR STORY........ROYALTY@MYEXCEL.COM

4
RIGHT ROAD, WRONG TIME
Kelvin E. Mattair

Whoever made the statement, "The youngest child has it easy growing up in life," was lying! I grew up in Madison, Florida, behind two older brothers and two older sisters, not to mention the fact that my brothers were all-star athletes. One sister that was also athletic, smart, and full of charisma, and then my other sister was just freaking beautiful!

During my high school years, I found it very hard to squeeze somewhere into these dynamic characteristics that my siblings possessed; so I decided to create my own road and leave my own legacy. I was great at basketball, football, and baseball, but could never stay focused enough to be successful in school at any of the sports. After a couple of failed attempts, due to my lack of maturity, I started looking down on myself as a failure and a disappointment to my family. So I packed my bags, all my precious memories, put the few dollars in my pocket, and threw them in the backseat of my 1987 Chevy Caprice Classic searching for the quickest road out of Madison. After a few brief goodbyes to some of my closest friends and seeing the love of my life at the time, shattered my heart into a million pieces, I chose I-75 South, the road that I thought would lead me to greatness. *Right Road, Wrong Time.*

Finally, after arriving in Gainesville, Florida, I wasted no time in making myself known in this wonderful town. My first objective was to reconnect with my old friends, from previous years of when I used to visit Gainesville. After solidifying a close group of friends (entourage), I felt more comfortable and not alone in the town. A year or two passed, and I went to the best place I knew I could make an impact—West Side Park Basketball Courts. While playing basketball for several hours, I was approached by an individual who wasn't too fond of my great basketball skills. We began to get into an altercation, and I slung the ball towards him and hit him directly in the face. He stormed towards my direction, with malice in his eyes, and like any normal person would do, I attempted to defend myself. I was unaware, but I was being attacked from the rear also; his brother struck me on the side of my head causing instant damage, leaving me knocked unconscious. I collapsed to the court immediately, and I woke up hours later, next to my vehicle. I never expected to be in this position while playing basketball. After this incident, it was definitely an eye opener for me, but I remained focused and refused to fail in making my mark in this town. My friends decided to relocate to Jacksonville, Florida, where I was sure to follow. *Right Road, Wrong Time.*

While visiting my friends in Jacksonville, I found myself starting to gamble frequently and began raking in some extra cash. On this particular night, my bad habits would eventually catch up with me. I begin gambling around 8:30 a.m. and found myself finishing about 1:30 the next morning. Feeling a little better, with cash bulging out of my pockets, I proceeded to my friend's workplace to boast about how much cash I had recently won while gambling. We laughed and frolicked around the store eagerly waiting for him to finish his shift. After my friend was finished with his shift, we departed from the store in separate vehicles. He led the way back to the apartment.

Upon arriving at the gates, I was two minutes behind my friend because of a traffic light, I jumped out of the car dressed in my black Jordan shoes, Dickie shorts hanging off my butt, an all black T-shirt, pocket full of dollar bills, Subway bag in my right hand, and a drink in my left hand. As I walked into the apartment, I noticed two individuals approaching very fast to my left with faces covered in black ski masks, carrying two wood grain AK-47's. I immediately stopped in my tracks. One individual shouted, "Get on the ground," while the other individual shouted, "Give me the money." I replied by asking, "What money?"

The next thing I knew, I was struck across the head with the tip of the barrel of the AK-47. With blood racing down my face, I wasted no time digging into my cash filled pockets and throwing the wad of cash at the masked men. They left me there on the ground shouting, "Don't move until we leave, or we will shoot you." As I laid face first on the pavement, I eventually crawled into the apartment on my knees, blinded by the blood on my face, screaming for help, but my friends were nowhere to be found. Fortunately, they saw the robbery in progress and proceeded to get the security guard while it was happening. After being bandaged up by the local paramedics, I wasted no time in traveling back to Gainesville that same night and telling myself I must get back to where I'm comfortable. *Right Road, Wrong Time*.

A few years had passed and after several negative events that took place that put me in situations where I didn't want to be, at this time, I can finally attest to my past mishaps. My title, *Right Road, Wrong Time*, has significant meaning as it relates to what I have learned in life. *Right Road* signifies my belonging in life, my destination, my attempts to be as great as my siblings, my willingness to change, and become a better person. *Wrong Time* signifies my lack of knowledge, education, my selfishness, my arrogance, and the biggest of all, my immaturity.

I made my peace with God and asked for His forgiveness in all my past negative ways, begging him to bring me through the storm. After praying to the Lord for months and years, He finally sent me a beautiful daughter, Kamiya Alyssa Mattair, who has been my motivation to change my outlook on life and progress in a positive manner. God also sent me the most beautiful person I have ever seen, hailing from Alice Springs, Australia. She is my best friend, my confidant, my better half, my protector, my wife, and all the reasons why I should be a better man: Brittney Lee Mattair.

My advice to anyone who is trying to make a change in their lives: Make sure you have the *right time* to go along with that *right road* you are attempting to travel. God bless you all.

Kelvin E. Mattair
Email: kmattair@hotmail.com

MY THOUGHTS

How did this story impact you mentally?

_____
_____
_____
_____

These are the people that I will talk to if I am faced with what this author was faced with:

_____
_____
_____
_____

These are the people that I need to reach out to that may be struggling with what this author struggled with but don't have a clue that they can overcome it:

_____
_____
_____
_____

Self Motivation

I _____ understand that knowledge itself holds no power, until it is applied to our lives through our actions. I can overcome this seemingly insurmountable odd because I am Royalty from birth, making me ruler over my decisions. I will no longer live my life doubting what I am capable of overcoming.

YOU CAN CHANGE A LIFE AS WELL BY SHARING YOUR STORY……..ROYALTY@MYEXCEL.COM

5
A FEMALE ATHLETE DEALING WITH DISAPPOINTMENT
Tameika Ashley Jonas

I was born in Fairbanks, Alaska, and when I was a child, it was very interesting explaining to my fellow classmates about where I was born, and most of them didn't believe me. I was a military baby, and at the time of my birth my father, David Jonas, and my mother, Gwen Jonas, were stationed there. Growing up with the majority of my life in Tampa, Florida, I had a very good childhood. I was very blessed with parents that made certain that I was taken care of and had the best education possible.

Throughout my whole life, I have been in sports and have continued to do so in college. I can't remember when I didn't participate in a sport. I was either involved in softball, basketball, or dance. When I went to high school, I knew I would have to try out for the softball team to prove myself because as usual, I was the only African-American competing. God truly blessed me because I was granted an opportunity to be on the Varsity Squad and the lead-off batter.

During my freshman year, I really put up numbers for my team and continued to try and lead by example. My sophomore year came around, and it was time for softball tryouts again, but this time we had a new coach. After tryouts, they always display a list that tells you who is on the team or not. I looked down the list once, then twice, no Tameika Jonas, the only returner not to be granted on the team. Words could not explain how I felt. Clearly, my fellow teammates didn't understand and neither did the parents. This state of affairs was brought up to the Athletic Director because many people had concerns about me not playing and wanted answers. The new coach really didn't have an explanation and just said I didn't fit in the program. I was so mad but continued my school year, ran track, and made it to regionals.

Junior year came around, and it was time for softball tryouts again. I battled back and forth as to whether I wanted to go out there, but the spirit told me to continue doing what I love. I ended up making the team but sat the whole season. I just wanted to quit because I felt like I was on the team just because he didn't want to go through any problems again. When my senior year came around, and he was fired, I realized that prayer really works. I ended up starting, and receiving "first team all conference" for Hillsborough County.

With prayer and hard work, I was granted a scholarship to Bethune-Cookman University on a full ride which means BCU was paying for my whole education. Also, what helped me get to that point was being successful in the classroom, making good grades, and paying attention. As many people know, in high school if you do not make those grades, you will be ineligible to participate in sports. In college, it's serious because if you are part of a collegiate team and you do not make the grades, you will become ineligible to play and will be on probation with the possibility of being kicked off the team. So I knew I had to continue to do the same things that I had done in high school. I wanted to make certain that I would be able to continue to do what I love doing, and that's playing softball.

Through my freshman year of playing ball, I went through a lot of trials and tribulations. I was at a point where I was questioning my faith of being there, and I just wanted to give up and go back home. I had been in a dark place because I felt like ball was not what I expected. I disliked the coach, and she didn't really favor me. We would get into many arguments, and I found myself not respecting her as a coach or as a person. I hated the person I had become, and I wanted out.

At the end of each season, a meeting is scheduled with you and the coaches to talk about your scholarship, and to determine if you are being granted your scholarship back. I knew going into this meeting that I was not going to be granted a scholarship, and that I would be moving back home and probably going to the community college in Tampa. She began to talk. She told me that she believed in me, saw potential, and wanted me back in the program. My scholarship was dropped from a full ride to fifty percent, and the reason was because now I had to prove to her that I wanted to be a part of this program. I didn't know what to say because I knew I was going home, but God does things in your life to make you realize you have a purpose for something.

Walking out of that office really opened my eyes, and I realized that I had another chance to prove to not only family, but also my coaches, teammates, and myself, that I wanted to be there.

My sophomore year for ball came around, and I can truly say I was at peace with myself which allowed me to have a great relationship with my coach and teammates. As a result, I was granted more money for my scholarship and respect. I had a goal – that before I was done with playing softball, I wanted to win the Mid-Eastern Athletic Conference (MEAC) Championship. This is such an accomplishment in college, to win a championship for your division. My senior year came, and we were named MEAC Champions. It was the best feeling in the world!

Always remember that no matter where you are, anything can happen, in a quick second. I ended up unjustly in jail by a situation that I had no control over. I was charged with a felony against an officer and disorderly conduct. I knew walking into that jail that my life was over, but God does amazing things and has things planned for you and me. I ended up posting bail, and on top of that, my charges were expunged which means everything was erased from my records. I have really grown from these adverse situations, and it really has made me into the person I am today. The people you hang around can make the difference in everything you do. I had always heard that growing up, but it never hit home until I became an adult myself.

No matter what your dreams or ambitions are, just put your trust in God and things will happen. He already has a plan for you, but be assured that it won't always be easy because you will have trials and tribulations. From the many things I have been through, I almost gave up, but because of my strength and faith, I was blessed with a four-year-degree from Bethune-Cookman University in Physical Education and granted Certification in Teaching.

You will have people enter your life, but you have to choose who is there for a reason or a season.

Tameika Ashley Jonas
Email: Tameikajonas@yahoo.com

MY THOUGHTS

How did this story impact you mentally?
_____
_____
_____
_____

These are the people that I will talk to if I am faced with what this author was faced with:
_____
_____
_____
_____

These are the people that I need to reach out to that may be struggling with what this author struggled with but don't have a clue that they can overcome it:
_____
_____
_____
_____

Self Motivation

I _____ understand that knowledge itself holds no power, until it is applied to our lives through our actions. I can overcome this seemingly insurmountable odd because I am Royalty from birth, making me ruler over my decisions. I will no longer live my life doubting what I am capable of overcoming.

YOU CAN CHANGE A LIFE AS WELL BY SHARING YOUR STORY……..ROYALTY@MYEXCEL.COM

6
BELIEVE IN HIS PLAN
Craig Wilson

In order to remain focused and active, life requires us to create goals and dreams. However, it is also vital to keep our minds open for opportunities that lead us to true joy and the fulfillment God intends for us. My life continues to be an incredible journey, enduring experiences that seem random and hurtful, until their purposes are revealed down the road.

I knew great love and support from a large, close-knit family that celebrated every holiday together. I remember being encouraged from my earliest days to succeed in school and athletics. I excelled in both, and like so many other children, had "dreams of greatness." Of course, I had no idea what exactly I would be doing; only that I would be exceptionally good at it, which in turn would make me rich.

During my childhood, I periodically attended Sunday school but was never strongly encouraged to pray or attend church. God was real to me, but in a general, loving sense; not as an active part of my life. I was skeptical about religion itself because of the hypocrisy I saw in the actions of many of the practicing Christians I knew.

Despite a fairly stable childhood and a loving family, I began drinking alcohol and then smoking marijuana around the age of fourteen. For reasons I still do not fully understand, the drinking and drugs became a larger and larger part of my life. During that period, I took perilous risks, including unprotected sex, and many hours behind the wheel, and as a passenger, while drinking. My schoolwork and family relationships suffered. There was a period, when I was seventeen that I was constantly skipping school and moved in with a girlfriend.

After high school, when I came to the realization that I had ruined my chance to attend the Coast Guard Academy, I made the decision to enlist in the Coast Guard, in order to remove myself from the community where I had made so many bad decisions. Because I finished at the top of my boot camp company, I was allowed to choose any available duty station for my first assignment. I chose a ship based in Honolulu.

Many days for a young enlisted man entail mundane tasks, like cleaning floors, and painting the ship. Since my father taught me to take pride and shine in any job I performed, I excelled in military life. I continued to be given roles of responsibility, like various gun crews, torpedo tube crewman, helicopter tie-down crew, and lead seaman (quasi-supervisor). One of the keys to my successes in life has always been my willingness to learn new tasks, often by helping others. The Coast Guard first taught me that the help I gave to those around me (that many people saw, and continue to see, as weakness), at some later point benefitted me.

The friendships I made with my coworkers helped me choose my next duty station in Clearwater, Florida. After moving to Clearwater (shortly after my 21st birthday), I participated with some of my Coast Guard friends in hanging a Coast Guard flag on a construction crane while intoxicated. As a result, we were restricted to the base with ten-hour workdays, six days per week for forty-five days. On one of our "free Sundays," my coconspirator's girlfriend visited him at the base. She was on the way home with her friend after leaving the beach. Her friend happened to be the woman I fell madly in love with and married less than a year later.

If I can point to a single thing in my life that has brought me to believe in God, it is the growth and boundless love I have experienced since meeting Amy. We were just kids when we met. I was twenty-one, and Amy was nineteen. Making the decision and commitment to spend the rest of our lives together at that age was overconfident and naïve since we had so little life experience. Little did we know how much experience life was about to give us.

Two months before our wedding, after having one of my testicles removed because of a suspicious painful lump, I was diagnosed with cancer and was told to prepare for more surgery and treatment. Because of the type of cancer, Amy and I had to end our honeymoon early in order for me to return for surgery to remove all the lymph nodes in my abdomen. I thought I handled pain well, but nothing prepares you for the agony of being cut open from your sternum to your waist.

After the surgery, I was sent from Clearwater to San Antonio, Texas, to undergo further evaluation and to begin chemotherapy. The time away from each other during this trying time in our lives became a nightmare for Amy and me. While undergoing chemotherapy, we also confirmed that I was now unable to father children, one of the dreams we had discussed during our honeymoon. We had chosen names for a boy and girl.

I survived the cancer, and a few years later, I left the Coast Guard against the advice of nearly everyone around me. I felt I was destined for something bigger and did not want to be separated from my wife again.

I was hired as a Disease Intervention Specialist at the Health Department. My interviewing and investigative skills were utilized to locate individuals infected with or exposed to sexually transmitted diseases. The wide array of people encountered in this line of work requires the ability to be non-judgmental regarding drug use, sexual preferences, and illegal activity. This is when I first began to see how my life's experiences had prepared me to be helpful for others.

As my confidence increased, I become more active in providing outreach testing and then facilitating a human immunodeficiency virus (HIV) support group. Again, my experience of battling a life-threatening illness prepared me to empathize on a level that helped me to connect with others who were suffering.

As I grew older, I matured enough to agree to in-vitro fertilization from a sperm donor to have a baby with my wife. It was an expensive and frustrating process before we were finally able to get pregnant. At twenty-three weeks, for no apparent reason, our baby girl died. No pain I had ever endured hurt as badly as losing our baby and also seeing the heartbreak Amy suffered as a result.

On the day our baby girl was due to be born, our son was conceived. Our family has been through horrendous struggles dealing with his Tourette Syndrome, but our appreciation for having a living child has often been the only thing that has pulled us through.

My experiences with losing a child and learning to cope with a special needs child have helped me be more supportive of other families, both for my employees and for clients in the Healthy Start Programs where I have worked for the last ten years.

I love how my life is developing. God will continue to give me the tools to help others and to be rewarded through the love and support I am blessed to be able to provide. If not for the trials and suffering in my life, I could not have the appreciation I have for the truly good things in life and would not feel as accomplished because of the depth of connection I can make with others.

Love who you are, and appreciate all your experiences. Share yourself with those around you, and know that God uses every one of us, if we allow Him to.

Please look for my book of cultural exploration and personal growth titled, *I am Today*, due out in fall 2011.

Craig Wilson
Email: alw_tcw@comcast.net

MY THOUGHTS

How did this story impact you mentally?

_____
_____
_____
_____

These are the people that I will talk to if I am faced with what this author was faced with:

_____
_____
_____
_____

These are the people that I need to reach out to that may be struggling with what this author struggled with but don't have a clue that they can overcome it:

_____
_____
_____
_____

Self Motivation

I _____ understand that knowledge itself holds no power, until it is applied to our lives through our actions. I can overcome this seemingly insurmountable odd because I am Royalty from birth, making me ruler over my decisions. I will no longer live my life doubting what I am capable of overcoming.

YOU CAN CHANGE A LIFE AS WELL BY SHARING YOUR STORY……..ROYALTY@MYEXCEL.COM

7
JOURNEY TO A CONQUERING, OVERCOMING, & TRIUMPHANT SPIRIT
Edna Haynes-Turner

Life has been a journey—not a destination. Often times, one challenge in a journey will take an individual to a life changing juncture in his or her life. My destiny into greatness and a triumphant spirit required much. And today, I am grateful and blessed for every facet of the journey that has facilitated my process into "a vessel that God can use in the earth."

From around the ages of four to eight-years-old, I was molested by two male family members. I had shared the experiences with my mother before she passed, with my sister, Evelyn, and with my pastor. Sharing with them was not to assess blame. I chose to forgive, and I did not choose to embrace bitterness. Forgiveness liberated and allowed me to catapult to a "God-ordained destiny of greatness." I chose to share so that my heart, mind, and spirit could experience wholeness and liberation.

As I grew spiritually, I became aware of the pain and emptiness that were hidden inside of me. I had housed so much into emotional pockets in an effort to appear and feel that I had it "all together." Those four years of being violated, adversely shaped and affected the rest of my life. Those years created a young, violated, and emotionally damaged Edna that spoke to my mind, heart, and spirit. And unfortunately, I believed her for sixty years of my life. That voice spoke convincingly to me that I was not valued because of all those things that happened in my life. Thus, I believed the voice.

The voice continued throughout my childhood, teenage, and adult life. Every single personal and professional choice or relationship was filtered through the voice of a young, violated, and an emotionally damaged Edna. As a result, I did not feel or know that I deserved the absolute best that life offered. Yes, I was always a high achiever, academically and socially, but in the midst of all of the many achievements, the little girl inside of me was convinced that she really was not all that, and someone was going to find out. That was a frightening and insecure way to live. However, I wore the mask extremely well. It was custom made, and my insecurities were never seen. However, recently, I became weary of the emotional pockets, and the heavy mask. My heart, mind, and spirit began the journey to divine freedom and wholeness.

The journey to freedom and wholeness began with a request I made from God. *Father, what is wrong? Help me to know the Edna that you created me to be.* He let me know that all that He allowed to happen in my life was not designed to kill or destroy me but to create me into a vessel of honor for His kingdom use. He (God) took me back . . . for my last journey as a reminder of the triumphant spirit that He placed in me for His purpose. It was an emotional, cleansing, and empowering journey!

Rewind: The molestation and lack of validation led me on a journey of unbridled sexual experiences. However, I grew to know that it was not just a sexual experience for me. My heart, mind, and spirit were seeking love and validation. I wanted to be safe and secure, and everything in me believed that every meaningful relationship would provide that for me. In retrospect, love did come on a couple of occasions, but the young, violated, and an emotionally damaged Edna spoke and convinced me that I was not deserving of such a person in my life. I believed the voice. I believed the lie.

Rewind: Revisiting my journey allowed me to be reminded of the experience where I was brutally beaten, traumatized, and left beside the road. The reminder of the experience still hurts, but the thing that hurt the most was that those who avowed love for me said that, "You probably did something that caused him to do it." It took me days to recover, but during that experience the young, violated, and emotionally damaged Edna spoke again, convincing me that they were probably right. I believed the voice. Once again I placed the pain, hurt, and disappointment into one of my emotional pockets . . . shifted my "proverbial mask" and continued my journey. No one ever knew, except for me, how I was affected. Remember, my mask was custom made.

Rewind: I have seldom in my life, personally or professionally, attempted to "take back" anything that was taken from me. I simply didn't have the fight inside of me. In almost every facet of my life, I didn't know nor feel that I was of great value and would relinquish or compromise. Once again, no one, except for me, knew that. The emotional deoxyribonucleic acid, or DNA, that had been mapped into my being during the ages of four to eight and the young, violated, and emotionally damaged Edna had convinced me that my value was fleeting and transitory. My petition to God was that I wanted to be free and whole, and I wanted my heart to be healed from all pain, hurts, and disappointments. I wanted to trust my heart to giving and receiving love. It has been a long and tumultuous journey, but I would not change one single experience of my sixty-one years of living. My journey to a triumphant spirit has given me great revelation to the person God has created me to be. God, I thank you!

Years ago, God's word said to my heart that He had covered me from the time that I was in my mother's womb, and I, Edna, am fearfully and wonderfully made. He said that even before the earth was formed that I, Edna, was on His mind. I am grateful that God pushed the rewind button of my life. And today, I am able to unconditionally love, forgive, and be compassionate to those who hurt and abused me. Today, I am able to express the God-kind of confidence that I shall never say "Yes" to the young, violated, and emotionally damaged Edna. I know that she will speak again, but I will be able to say to her, "Your voice is silenced." I embrace everything that God allowed in my life because I now "know in my knower" that I was created by God with a conquering, overcoming, and triumphant spirit.

My words to the kings and queens of the world: Know that the God who created everything that was and is, not only created, but breathed His Spirit into each of us, and He has a plan and purpose for every single one of us. Embrace the journey, know you are loved, and fly, fly, fly into your God-ordained destiny.

Day by Day Celebrations
Scheduled to be published in 2011

Edna Haynes-Turner
Author, Motivational Speaker, Youth Advocate, and Contractor
TWTW: Talk With the Women, Inc., Tallahassee, FL

Email: etcelebration@yahoo.com

MY THOUGHTS

How did this story impact you mentally?
_____
_____
_____
_____

These are the people that I will talk to if I am faced with what this author was faced with:
_____
_____
_____
_____

These are the people that I need to reach out to that may be struggling with what this author struggled with but don't have a clue that they can overcome it:
_____
_____
_____
_____

Self Motivation

I _____ understand that knowledge itself holds no power, until it is applied to our lives through our actions. I can overcome this seemingly insurmountable odd because I am Royalty from birth, making me ruler over my decisions. I will no longer live my life doubting what I am capable of overcoming.

YOU CAN CHANGE A LIFE AS WELL BY SHARING YOUR STORY……..ROYALTY@MYEXCEL.COM

8
THAT CAN NEVER HAPPEN TO ME
At Least That's What I Thought
Marvin "Merv" Mattair

As a fourteen-year-old boy suffering with a sexually transmitted disease (STD) by the name of gonorrhea, it was a shock to me because young kids are immortal. Those types of things are not supposed to happen to us; at least that's what I thought!

As a young man growing up, I must say that I was blessed to have my birth parents to raise me and demonstrate the true meaning of home stability. My parents were awesome back then and still to this day, but there is one area that they lacked in, and that was the educating of me on the big word, sex. Was it fear they had that I may try it once they mentioned it? Was it because my dad did not have a dad to teach him, making it uncomfortable for him to talk to me about it? I am not sure what the delay was, but I was getting ready to find out from other sources.

I can remember being in middle school, and me and a few other guys would huddle around the guys who had the supply of dirty magazines. Now these magazines only had naked pictures of women and because the older guys liked them, I thought that I had to like it as well. I wanted to be a regular boy by fitting in to the point that I started holding on to them and showing them to others. It was starting to be a mental distraction because I wanted to see more.

Being the oldest son got me a few more privileges to hang out with my older cousins, go to the night parties, etc. I can recall going to parties at this building in my hometown, where a popular disc jockey (DJ) would come down and show the crowd a good time through his loud and updated music making the people want for more. When he would play songs like "Set it Off," we would all be on the dance floor doing the bus stop and other dances to sway with the rhythm of the beat. But when he played certain songs, the gestures of the crowd changed, and the lights got dimmer.

The older youth and some adults seemed to be having sex while dancing, while several younger youth, including myself, stood on the wall and looked on with possible curiosity. I attended that environment a few times. When those songs came on, requesting that the girls bend over and shake it or drop it like it's hot, I was right there in the midst of the crowd. I was normally sex dancing with an older girl because the girls my age were normally with an older guy. I started liking it for several reasons, but the main one being that it made me feel cool to be doing what several others were doing. It never failed that at least one of the older guys would be next to me dancing with a girl and giving me the thumbs up as if he was saying, "Do your thing lil man." So I was pumped up.

We, my boys and I, graduated from the little naked women magazines to the hardcore ones which displayed sexual acts between men and women and from there to videocassette recorder (VCR) tapes. Because I was exposed to the pictures, the videos, the conversations, and actions of older youth in my presence, I became sexually active. I did not know what I was doing, I just wanted to get the feeling that some of the older guys was talking about, not knowing that I was digging a ditch for myself. I kept all of my feelings about sex away from my parents because I did not feel comfortable telling them. I talked to older guys in the hood because I felt comfortable, and I did not have to watch what I said around them.

At the age of fourteen, due to my curiosity, my lack of knowledge with the use of contraceptives, my fearless mentality, and pressure from this world's sexual appetite, I was diagnosed with a case of gonorrhea. I can remember the day when I could not bear the pain anymore. I had to tell my mom because she was the one home at the time. Because of my embarrassment, I told her that I had been working out, and I must have pulled something, but it hurt real bad when I went to the bathroom and could she please take me to the doctor. My mom immediately uncovered that lie by looking me in the eyes and stating, "Boy don't lie to me, what have you been doing?" I then had to tell her, and then she got me seen by the doctor. When the doctor diagnosed me with that STD, I was very embarrassed and in so much pain from the procedure to test for it. I had seen the little STD slides that the school provided through a presentation trying to scare us youth, but those were only adults in those pictures, and I knew that it could not happen to me; at least I thought it couldn't happen to me.

Here are a few statistics that were pulled from The Center from Disease Control in an attempt to educate you more in depth:

- *Some 46% of all teens, ages 15-19, in the United States have had sex.*
- *Some 71.5 out of every 1,000 teenage girls, ages 15-19, became pregnant in the United States in 2006.*
- *The United States has the highest teen pregnancy rate by far compared to other countries.*
- *Only half the girls in the United States who become pregnant in high school graduate, and just 3% graduate from college by age 30.*
- *Nineteen million new STD infections occur in the United States every year.*
- *Nearly 50% of these new cases happen to young people between the ages of 15 and 24.*

Young people, I want you to know that your body is a temple that's worthy of being taken care of, but it first takes you mentally understanding that before you can really live up to it. You see, I was only diagnosed with gonorrhea, but who's to say that if you take that path that you'll not end up with acquired immune deficiency syndrome (AIDS)? My story is not embarrassing anymore for me to tell because I realized that we all go through stuff for a reason and when we keep it in, we may be missing out on the chance to save a life. The best way to keep from coming into contact with an STD or a baby is to say "No" to sexual intercourse. Yes, we as adults know the pressures that you are faced with through the music, the videos, the radio stations, the movies, and the commercials, but you have to be willing to listen to us and not lean on your own understanding.

Young ladies, walk with your heads held high because you are young queens. So walk like one, talk like one, dress like one, and refuse to lower your standards. You cannot continue to go around allowing anyone to treat you as a sex toy or just a chick on the side, and you take pleasure in it because the same things that are whispered in your ear, is more than likely, being whispered in another's ear as well. So wake up and take charge of your mind.

No, young men do not like using contraceptives, so the first chance that they get to remove it, they will. So stand up for yourself by realizing that you may get an STD, or you may get pregnant, and the little boy or grown man is not going to be there in the morning to change diapers or give milk to the baby, you are, and possibly your parents, not his.

Young men, when you read Mr. David Dukes story, that should let you know about the things that do not define a man. You have the chance to be that in which you are seeking, but you have to be willing to listen. As a father and husband now, I can tell you that there is no sustainability in being hard, being sexually active at an early age, or stressing to fit in. Being hard causes you to not want to listen, as if you have all of the answers. Being sexually active at a young age poses the risk of losing your life to an STD, or having a baby from someone that you were just playing around with and being forced to be a father when you're not prepared to be one. Stressing to fit in only causes you to be impulsive by doing everything that's new and popular without giving any thought as to how it will affect your future. There is nothing wrong with being a gentleman that's in control of his decisions. And there is nothing wrong with you saying "No" to sexual intercourse.

There are several ways to have fun as a youth without engaging in sexual acts, but it may take you changing your choice of musical artists, it may take you changing your group of peers, it may take you saying "No" on a daily basis, it may take you sitting in the front of the class, etc. But understand that nothing is going to change until you decide. The sexual music, commercials, movies, conversations, and so much more is going to continue to flow, but it's up to you, young king. The most important thing that all of you can do is practice ASAP (Always Say a Prayer).

Adults, I think that we can identify with how this world functions if our eyes are open. Our youth needs us, but we must be willing to stand in the gap for them like a lot of us are already doing. This world is fighting against us and "Yes" sometimes it knocks us down, causing us to fall to our knees, but we must get back up quick. I guess it would be easier for us if adults would just stop promoting and making music with sexual content. If they stop showing half dressed women dancing on television at times when our youth are tuned in, if they stop placing sexual scenes in commercials, or if they stop advertising condoms as if they're some sort of sports equipment, but that's not going to happen because we, as adults, take pleasure in some of that content, giving it validation and support.

Those statistics are troubling to me because the easily assessable sexual content is doing more harm to our youth compared to us, so I ask, "Who is actually the targeted audience?" You see, I realized that negative statistics is an issue for some, but a dollar sign for others. Parents, we can no longer get caught saying years later, "I wish I would have," when we can do right now. So let's set some standards to say that although this world may accept specific content, it will not be allowed in my house. We will never be perfect in that area, but we can at least try. Let's find the time to talk with our kids about these sorts of issues instead of letting the world do it for us. We are the change, but it's only when we decide.—Peace & Ubuntu.

Marvin Terrell Mattair
"BKA" Merv
Author, Motivational Speaker, Youth Advocate, and Contractor

Email: royalty@myexcel.com
Website: www.kingsqueens.org

MY THOUGHTS

How did this story impact you mentally?
_____
_____
_____
_____

These are the people that I will talk to if I am faced with what this author was faced with:
_____
_____
_____
_____

These are the people that I need to reach out to that may be struggling with what this author struggled with but don't have a clue that they can overcome it:
_____
_____
_____
_____

Self Motivation

I _____ understand that knowledge itself holds no power, until it is applied to our lives through our actions. I can overcome this seemingly insurmountable odd because I am Royalty from birth, making me ruler over my decisions. I will no longer live my life doubting what I am capable of overcoming.

YOU CAN CHANGE A LIFE AS WELL BY SHARING YOUR STORY……..ROYALTY@MYEXCEL.COM

9
THE AMAZING JOURNEY OF HEALING
Angela Y. Hodge

Oftentimes, I was faced with decisions. There were choices I had to make. No matter how hard it seemed, I knew deep down in the deep parts of my being that I had to stand on truth and believe it would all work for my good. Many times, I had to stand alone, and some days, fear would overtake me. Standing was hard, yet I managed to make it.

Through all the shame, lies, and rejection, there was always a voice that would softly whisper to me, "It's through your pain that you gain strength." But where would my strength come from? After many sleepless nights, the answer came, "You gain strength from My word." It was in the Bible that I found hope, strength, and faith to endure the journey. It was there, in His Word, that I found peace to press on. It was there, in His unchanging Word, that I found joy to overcome all of the fiery darts. Yes, it was indeed there, in His loving Word, that I found comfort in knowing that the Holy Ghost would lead and direct my path.

So many people questioned my belief and faith in God. There was indeed a purpose and a plan for my life. Greater and deeper character needed to be born. But oh, on a hot, summer day in June 1995, an illness hit me. I went back and forth to the doctor, and I have never been eager for doctor visits. During those visits, I stared at the wall and waited patiently for the results. Confused and worried, the tears would fall from my face as I sat there listening to the air conditioner rumbling like a mighty, rushing wind.

For two years, I went to get check-ups every three months. Three years after that, those check-ups became required every six months. I was becoming burned out from crying within, but I still called on Jesus! I petitioned him, "Lord, it's in your hands, and I trust you! Healing is what I need! Please restore my soul?" Little did I know that He had already stepped in, healed my body, and set me free!

All I needed was a little faith! Those check-ups were cancelled. Worthy is thy name and prayer does change things! I fasted, I prayed, I overcame that sickness, and I survived that test. Some nights were cold and lonely. Some days I felt blue. My hair fell out in patches. My legs would swell in pain. But, day after day, I held on, as I would quote my favorite Scripture to help ease the tension:

> *I waited patiently for the Lord; and he inclined unto me, and heard my cry, He brought me up also out of a horrible pit, out of the miry clay, and set my foot upon a rock, and established my goings.*
> ~Psalms 40:1-2

I say to you, forgive, so that your healing can begin! When we do not forgive, it blocks our blessings. Speak life over every adverse or challenging situation in your life! Hold on. Don't give up. When we become weak, it is important that we stand in the strength of "the Great I Am" who lives within us. Keep the faith! When you activate your faith, do not waver or become double-minded, all things are possible through Christ Jesus. In total darkness, He will shine His light and give you the strength to start over again! For He is our healer!

> *Who forgiveth all thine iniquities who healeth all thy diseases who redeemeth thy life from destruction; who crowneth thee with loving-kindness and tender mercies?"*
> ~Psalms 103: 3-4

Be encouraged! It's through our pain that we gain strength!

Day to Day Encouragement
Poems by: Angela Y. Hodge
Expected release date is late 2011
Email: ayhodge69@yahoo.com

MY THOUGHTS

How did this story impact you mentally?
_____
_____
_____
_____

These are the people that I will talk to if I am faced with what this author was faced with:
_____
_____
_____
_____

These are the people that I need to reach out to that may be struggling with what this author struggled with but don't have a clue that they can overcome it:
_____
_____
_____
_____

Self Motivation

I _____ understand that knowledge itself holds no power, until it is applied to our lives through our actions. I can overcome this seemingly insurmountable odd because I am Royalty from birth, making me ruler over my decisions. I will no longer live my life doubting what I am capable of overcoming.

YOU CAN CHANGE A LIFE AS WELL BY SHARING YOUR STORY……..ROYALTY@MYEXCEL.COM

10
SAVED FOR GREATNESS
Gerald Bullocks

To all my young brothers and sisters, I hope these words of encouragement will touch your lives and lead you to a path of righteousness. In addition, I hope my testimony will bring joy, good health, and good spirit in your life. The road of life can be difficult due to obstacles; for example, I was once headed down the road of self-destruction as well as death. In many situations of life, you must change your attitude and move forward in order for positive outcomes to follow.

I was born and raised in Cincinnati, Ohio. Comparable to a lot of children, I came from a good family which had occasional problems such as greed, hatred, recovery, and selfishness. My mother had nine kids, and I was child number eight. For five years, I was the baby until the last child was born. My little brother, I nicknamed him Scooby.

As a young child, I was sick, so my activities were limited compared to other children my age. I was diagnosed with epilepsy and suffered from seizures. Normal children could play sports, jump rope, climb trees, and participate in other childhood activities, but I couldn't. Even though, my parents tried to prevent me from playing sports, my passion for playing sports became too great. Consequently, I began to sneak behind my parents' back and play sports because I was extremely good at it. The sports I played were baseball and football. Personally, sports seemed to be a vacation from home.

The good thing is that with family, unity changed situations. My father and grandfather were the love of my life, but do not get me wrong because I love my mother and grandmother as well. In some families, men are the role models and will try to show the younger boys how to act and make them aware of what hidden rules to follow as well as what fun games to play such as football, baseball, and basketball. So that is why I share such a strong bond with my father and grandfather.

My father's mother, Grannie, treated me differently than she treated my baby brother, who was ten months older than me. The last three of my siblings were raised by Grannie, so that was how the living arrangements were structured. I was considered the "black sheep" of the family because I resembled my mother so much, and my grandmother always made me remember it. For example, when Grannie disciplined me, she would chastise me more severely than the other children.

In the back of my mind, I kept telling myself that when I grew up, my children would never get treated like this, and I asked God to bless her soul. During one Christmas, she bought my other two brothers some toys and got me nothing. Grannie was so hateful towards me that she would try to manipulate my two other brothers to isolate me. When they were playing with their toys, she told them not to allow me to play with their toys. Even though I had no toys to play with, my heart was filled with enjoyment to see my brother, Doug, play with his race car set. Of course, I displayed a smile for everyone, so that they would not see my pain, but the pain became too much. One day, I ran away from my grandmother and straight to my mother's home.

My mother was a totally different person from my Grannie because she showed me how much she loved me. I was allowed to stay up all night long, and party all night long, as long as I followed three conditions: Remain in school, stay out of trouble, and make good grades. My school attendance and grades were good, but I could not stay out of trouble. I did get in trouble, and I began sneaking around with girls, smoking weed, and drinking beer. All of these factors were inherited because everyone in my family experienced one, the other, or all of the above. I supported my habits through doing odd jobs for different people. People often said that, "What you do in the dark will come to light," and it did.

My fourteen-year-old girlfriend found out that she was pregnant, and it shocked everyone. My family did not believe in abortions; on the other hand, her family believed in abortions, so my pregnant girlfriend moved in with my mom and me. This was challenging for her, too, because she had to continue her education as well.

Guess what? My girlfriend had twin girls. I was the proudest father in the world and loved my girls, unconditionally. Surprisingly, after a few months, my girlfriend was pregnant again with another set of twin girls. The situation was getting critical because my family's size got bigger, and I needed money extremely fast in order to take care of them. Eventually, I started selling weed but because of my excessive habit of smoking weed, I wasn't making any money. I smoked my own supply.

A neighborhood thug said, "Young man, the only way that you are going to make any money is to sell something you do not use." I did not use cocaine, so he gave me my first package. The more he gave me, the more I sold, and that meant progress. Ultimately, I got out on my own, my own dope, and my own money which meant I owed nobody nothing. I was able to pay my rent, buy food, clothes, cars, jewelry, shoes, and especially buy my children all of the gifts my grandmother did not buy me for Christmas. For the first time in my life, I felt like I was on top of the world; not knowing that I was poisoning my own people as well as not being a good father towards my children.

As the years passed, my girlfriend kept having more children, and we eventually had eight children. I had eight girls and no boys. I began to second guess the paternity of my children because I stayed in the streets doing so much hustling that I began to feel as though someone else was having sex with my girlfriend.

Women were obsessed with me because of my extravagant lifestyle and my large amounts of cash. I was the man they wanted to be with, and they did not care that I had a girlfriend with children as long as I kept dishing out money and other materialistic goods to them. My mind was so confused because the lifestyle in which I was living was not right; it broke all laws, and it also went against every one of God's principles that I had been taught. I knew that I had been brought up in the church and thought about giving back to the community. I began to weigh my advantages and disadvantages of sin and how it would affect eternal sanctity. Two questions kept popping up in my mind: How wrong was I for poisoning my fellow man? What could I do to change the situation from negative to positive?

More bad news came when I got busted for selling crack and was facing thirty-three to sixty years in the federal prison system. For the first time in years, I got on my knees and prayed. While in jail, I constantly attended Bible study and church. Other inmates would talk about me and try to discourage me with words like, "God is not going to help you, and you are going to get twenty-five years in prison." I refused to claim that in my mind, body, soul, and spirit because God is good and merciful. He just wanted me to get a wake-up call and realize that His way is the only true way for eternal happiness. God wanted me to serve Him, worship Him, and give Him my time; on the other hand, Satan was playing games with my life because I allowed him to do so.

After two months of being locked up, I made bond. Instead of running to the church to seek God, I ran back to the streets and sought Satan. The only thing that changed my life was a brush with death. After returning to the streets, I got robbed, shot four times, and was left for dead. But once again, God stepped in and saved my life. God was not ready for me yet, and he wanted me to learn from my mistakes. I recovered from the gunshot wounds and was sent to jail. I was given a court date, and at my court appearance, the judge gave me five years but released me after serving eighteen months. I decided to relocate from my hometown of Cincinnati and move to Florida, where I met a strong, Christian woman. She helped me to take steps toward God, and I truly thank her for that. God came first, and he led me to my queen, Penny Mitchell, who I love with all of my heart because through my Savior, I am truly blessed and saved.

So if you are out there living the wrong type of lifestyle, please change and "give it up to Christ." He loves you, and you need to love Him back.

Email: Gerald.bullocks@yahoo.com

MY THOUGHTS

How did this story impact you mentally?
_____
_____
_____
_____

These are the people that I will talk to if I am faced with what this author was faced with:
_____
_____
_____
_____

These are the people that I need to reach out to that may be struggling with what this author struggled with but don't have a clue that they can overcome it:
_____
_____
_____
_____

Self Motivation

I _____ understand that knowledge itself holds no power, until it is applied to our lives through our actions. I can overcome this seemingly insurmountable odd because I am Royalty from birth, making me ruler over my decisions. I will no longer live my life doubting what I am capable of overcoming.

YOU CAN CHANGE A LIFE AS WELL BY SHARING YOUR STORY……..ROYALTY@MYEXCEL.COM

11
PERSONAL STRUGGLES OF A FATHERLESS GIRL
Meshalene Love-Taylor

I was born Meshalene T. Daniels, to Mr. and Mrs. Willie Daniels, on April 3, 1975, in Orlando, Florida, and my birth was like any other ordinary delivery. I was a healthy, happy, and crying baby girl being welcomed by two proud and loving parents. At least, that's what every child expects when they are born, but little did I know that my parents were going through a very ugly divorce, a divorce that would leave me fatherless for the rest of my life.

I'm the oldest of three children that my mother had, one sister that resides in Tennessee, and one brother that resides in Florida. Growing up was not always easy for us, in fact, at times it was downright hard and painful. I saw my mother as a strong-minded black woman, and I realized later on in life just how much she underwent just to raise us. Our mother struggled and worked two jobs in order to support our family. I remember so many nights, when she thought we were all asleep; I could hear her crying in her room.

My living environment was not always stable because we moved around a lot, and sometimes in very unsafe places. Most of the time we were left all alone while she worked, and she depended on us to behave and be obedient. I know there were a lot of things my siblings and I could have done to make things more difficult for her, but we never did. We learned to keep fights and disagreements to a minimum because of our love for her, we didn't want to put more stress on her than she was already experiencing.

In society, many people feel a two parent family is not needed in order to raise a family successfully. In many cases, children are reared just fine without both parents, but for me, that was not always the case. Not having a father in my life growing up has definitely attributed to many difficulties that I've encountered with the opposite sex, making good choices, and stability. My last year of high school, I succumbed to pre-marital sex and got pregnant. I was never taught how to submit to the headship and directions from a man. My mother was always both my father and mother. She taught me how to be independent and strong when faced with life's struggles. So more often than not, when faced with an obstacle, I would always turn to her for guidance rather than my mate. This has always caused problems within my relationships.

Getting pregnant while still in school, caused me to lose my academic scholarship to college. I thought I had found true love, and I devastated my family because of it. I was never a problem child and was never one prone to trouble, but wanting to be accepted by my peers caused me to continue making bad decisions. At the age of nineteen, I got in trouble with the law, and that choice was something I will never be proud of. Making that one bad choice has caused me to lose out on so many things that I've wanted to do in life. Although that was many years ago, my rights have since been restored, and a full pardon has ensued. Whenever my record is pulled, I'm still faced with and will always be reminded of that bad decision. I constantly try to instill in my children not to succumb to peer pressure and to always, despite feeling different, make decisions based on what they know to be right.

These things that I have spoken of in my story have always been my *insurmountable odds*, but since that time, I have learned better ways to deal with life's troubles. And I have overcome a lot of self induced situations that I thought I would never be freed from. I have since opened two businesses in Madison, Florida. One of my businesses is named, T.D.M.D Financial Services, and we provide tax preparations and do payrolls. My other business is titled, Tax Doctor, M.D. & More, where we conduct drug screenings. I now manage accounts that I never thought in a million years I would receive.

My desire is that sharing my story will offer encouragement to you. Do not wallow in self pity as some have the custom of doing. When you fall, get back up, stand erect, brush yourself off, and continue on your course. People say all the time you never get a second chance to recover from a mistake, but I say second chances are only given to those who do not give up!

I'm living proof of it, thank you for reading.

Meshalene Love-Taylor
Email: taxdoctor.md@gmail.com

MY THOUGHTS

How did this story impact you mentally?
_____
_____
_____
_____

These are the people that I will talk to if I am faced with what this author was faced with:
_____
_____
_____
_____

These are the people that I need to reach out to that may be struggling with what this author struggled with but don't have a clue that they can overcome it:
_____
_____
_____
_____

Self Motivation

I _____ understand that knowledge itself holds no power, until it is applied to our lives through our actions. I can overcome this seemingly insurmountable odd because I am Royalty from birth, making me ruler over my decisions. I will no longer live my life doubting what I am capable of overcoming.

YOU CAN CHANGE A LIFE AS WELL BY SHARING YOUR STORY……..ROYALTY@MYEXCEL.COM

12
CHASING A DREAM
Marcus Hawkins

I am almost certain that there is no one who does not have a dream of becoming or attaining something greater than what they are or previously had. I think it goes without saying that this is a norm of life—to dream. My dream started when I was a young boy growing up in the projects, Jeanette Circle, Brooklyn Avenue, and wherever else time took me. Basketball was my thing, so I loved to dribble and play. In those days, there wasn't a neighborhood that was not sprinkled with a homemade rim and backboard. And if it was there, you were certain to find me, and the boys, grinding the pavement. So it was, basketball was my dream, and I dreamed of playing it one day for my career.

There I was a senior in high school with decisions. I had just had a successful junior basketball season and was a senior and leader on the team. It was only right that it be my year. However, it is rare that we make sound decisions at such a young age. I decided to play football. Although I do not regret the experience of playing, I do regret the time it took away from me furthering my basketball abilities. You have got to understand that football in Madison County is big! Almost every year our football team went deep into the playoffs, if not to the championship. That year, 1997, we went to the state final four which took us into December. Those of you who are hip to basketball know that December is almost the midpoint, and so here I was, a senior, with a slight chance of making an impression with only half a year left. What had I done to my dream?

With no college scholarship offers after I graduated from high school, I managed for two years at North Florida Community College. There, I would go to the gym and watch the women's basketball program.[1] Clyde Alexander, who was the coach at the time, allowed me to come in and shoot around. I still had a dream! I can remember well the day I walked into Coach's office, and he gave me the Blue Book (and no, not the Kelly Blue Book). The Blue Book was a book listing every junior and senior college, NCAA Division I, II, and III as well as NAIA Division I and II. I perused through Florida, Georgia, and Alabama, calling almost every school I thought would be willing to accept a boy chasing a dream. St. John's River Community College invited me for a try-out, but they didn't have scholarships. I couldn't afford that. Valdosta State allowed me to come to a try-out, but once again, no scholarships. As you can probably guess, my hopes were fading fast. There was one last call to North Georgia College and State University. A military school located in a place whose name I did not even know how to pronounce at the time. So I called. Coach Randy Dunn invited me up to a try-out. Unlike the other try-outs, I went to NGCSU, and they had some scholarships. And so my dream was becoming a reality or what I thought was my dream.

My career began at NGCSU in 2000. The summer of 2000, I graduated from NFCC and headed to Fort Knox, Kentucky, for Basic Camp. Not only had I found the door to my dream, but I also walked through that door with hopes of maybe enlisting in the United States Army as an officer after graduating. This would be my back-up plan in case my ultimate dream of playing basketball for a career fell through. I was now a full-time student at a senior military college playing basketball, when just six months earlier; I was stranded with no hope.

My NGCSU basketball career went by pretty well. Since I had gone to NFCC for two years full-time, I was only granted three years of eligibility. They were wonderful. It was the things off the court that rattled my dreams more than anything else. In January of 2002, my very first daughter was born (Makeela Ashe' Hawkins). This put things in perspective for me, and made it seem almost necessary that I fulfill that dream. In the summer between my second and third year, I experienced something that opened my eyes. There I was, a young boy from little ole Madison, Florida. I

---

[1] NFCC discontinued its men's basketball program in 1991-92.

was chasing a dream, and it was almost a reality. During that summer, I had gone to visit my dad. I stayed in Mrs. Green's Trailer Park (as did some of my other teammates). I came home to find that there was a big leak under my trailer. A pipe had burst. To top off my troubles, the burst pipe caused the hot water heater to run overtime. So not only did I have water problems, I now had electricity problems. I was now a college student, with a kid, barely making it with two bills totaling $1,000. How in the world would I manage? I did not know.

Over the course of the next month and a half, I spent nights here and there, with this friend and that friend. When I could not spend the night with a friend, I was forced to stay in our team locker room. There I was, almost 400 miles away from my hometown, with no place to stay. The water was fixed, but the lights were another story. So I was forced to use storm candles and the gas stove. How could something like this happen? Basketball was going well, I was getting close to graduation, and it seemed like my dream was about to become a reality. It had to become a reality because now my life was no longer about me but about my seed.

Eventually I got a roommate during my senior year, and so the burden was lifted slightly. My senior year was under way. Maybe basketball would lift my spirits because, after all, this was the dream I was chasing. However, that dream would have to wait. During a morning pre-season workout, I went up to block a shot and when I came down, my left knee felt funny. I went to the doctor and found out that I had cracked my patella. This injury put me out for seven weeks. I returned and finished my senior year. The only thing left was graduation, and then chasing that dream.

As my graduation neared, I began lining up some Continental Basketball Association (CBA) and Florida Basketball League (FBL) try-outs. There was only one try-out available, and it was on August tenth. Since my graduation, I had been unable to find a job in the north Georgia area. I can remember the night well. I was sitting alone and contemplating this dream I was chasing. How would my daughter make it while I chased this dream? I prayed. I can remember asking God clearly to open a door. I really did not want to go back to Madison, but I knew that my daughter was there, but not much opportunity. I knew that if I chased after this hoop dream, it would take me away from my daughter for a while. I put in an application at Madison County High School. I received a phone call stating that I had an interview on August tenth.

There I was, praying, asking God to open a door clearly before me. I had a dream, and I wanted to chase it. I wanted to be the first one from Madison to go and play professional basketball. I also had a daughter who needed her father. And so I prayed. I asked God to *lead me where He wanted me to go*. At that moment, I had no job, and if He gave me the job in Madison, I knew that it was my sign to serve Him. If He took me on this journey, chasing that dream, a hoop dream, then I would know it was His will. Before me stood a decision—accept the interview on August tenth or make the try-out on the same date. This was the dream. I was chasing a dream, a hoop dream (CADAHD). Was I really?

This entire NGCSU experience had actually not been about basketball. Yes, I had played and done very well, but all the while God was speaking to me. As a matter of fact, He was speaking to me before NGCSU, it was only magnified then. I began to see it. God was allowing these things in my life in order that I may realize what I was actually chasing. *I was not chasing a hoop dream; I was chasing a heavenly dream,* but a dream that God had implanted within me before my acknowledgement. All the while I was autographing CADAHD (Chasing a Dream, a Hoop Dream), when it was right, although the dream wasn't a hoop dream. It was a heavenly dream.

I am thankful for my Dahlonega experience. To me it was my wilderness. It was my period of testing. It was my forty years. As a pastor now, I look back and I'm thankful for every experience I had because it has allowed me to reflect on the hand of God at work in my life. Now I am on the right track, chasing the right dream—a heavenly dream!

Marcus Hawkins
Email: mhawk320@gmail.com

MY THOUGHTS

How did this story impact you mentally?
_____
_____
_____
_____

These are the people that I will talk to if I am faced with what this author was faced with:
_____
_____
_____
_____

These are the people that I need to reach out to that may be struggling with what this author struggled with but don't have a clue that they can overcome it:
_____
_____
_____
_____

Self Motivation

I _____ understand that knowledge itself holds no power, until it is applied to our lives through our actions. I can overcome this seemingly insurmountable odd because I am Royalty from birth, making me ruler over my decisions. I will no longer live my life doubting what I am capable of overcoming.

YOU CAN CHANGE A LIFE AS WELL BY SHARING YOUR STORY........ROYALTY@MYEXCEL.COM

13
FROM POVERTY to the PRESIDENT'S OFFICE
Leslie DeRenzo

I was born into a loving Christian Italian home, where my father was the breadwinner, and my mother was a homemaker. When I was twelve, we moved from New York to Florida. My father went from a well-paying job to working three jobs at very low pay. My parents modeled for their children a strong work ethic and strong faith in God. We never missed a meal, and they never missed a payment. Mom and Dad never spoke about financial issues but faithfully went about their daily work with joy and no complaints. Each of us (children) received a few dollars each week, and was taught to save some, and put some into the church offering plate.

After high school, I worked at a factory and took a few college classes, hoping to earn a degree which would help earn more money. After several years, I met Tone,' who had come from western Africa to attend college in the United States. He worked part-time and attended college classes. I was not working at the time but had some money saved to live on. We spent hours sharing our hopes and dreams. We both wanted to earn college degrees and have children. Tone' explained how we could get government assistance to help meet our goals.

We got married and lived in Section Eight housing in a tiny apartment. The projects were two blocks away, and the neighborhood men spent their days at the bar down the street. Tone' and I went dancing at the Blue Flame club on Saturday nights, two minutes away, and just across the railroad tracks. The neighborhood women hated me, as I had *taken one of their men*. I didn't care. I was in love and was going to have Tone's baby.

We applied for a government PELL grant to pay my college expenses. I began attending college full-time. We also received food stamps and free pre-natal care at the county health department. Once our daughter was born, the health department provided well-child care plus food and formula through the Women, Infants, and Children (WIC) Program. There was also free government surplus food from time to time. When our son was born, we continued receiving government help from all these programs. Many days, I wondered when we would get out of poverty and take care of ourselves. We did not like depending on the government.

After five years, Tone' and I graduated from college. He found a job in another city, and we moved. I also went to work full-time. We were finally independent of all government help! Our neighbor, Shirley, cared for the children in our rented home. She loved them like a grandmother, and we never worried about their well-being.

Tone's employer, a government contractor, had lay-offs from time to time. Tone's time came, and he was out of work. Tone' received unemployment compensation from the government for six months. Then, he found part-time jobs and attended college classes, hoping to go into teaching or the medical field, and at the same time, we sent his resume' out weekly in search of a new job. I had taken a job as a supervisor, and worked sixty hours a week. I also worked a part-time consulting job to bring in more money. We used credit cards to pay for a new refrigerator, and then got into a habit of using them for things we wanted but didn't need. We did not use wisdom in the use of credit. Tone's unemployment and my heavy work schedule continued for three and a half years. Yet, we never missed a meal and never missed a payment.

An opportunity for a job promotion came for me in another city. We moved to the Florida State Capitol, where I managed three offices as a District Manager. Tone' eventually went to work for another government contractor. By this time, our credit card bills were huge, $10,000. We had not been good stewards of our money. We made monthly payments of $1,000 and got out of credit card debt in ten months. We then bought expensive cars, another bad financial decision. We were back making $1,000 monthly payments, this time for cars that lost value the minute we bought them.

By now, our children were in high school, and we still lived in a rented house. Our credit card and automobile debts kept us from buying our own home. Instead, we were paying someone else's mortgage with rent payments. My personal financial goals were to begin giving ten percent of my income (the tithe) to God's work, begin investing money, and become totally debt free, except for a mortgage payment. I left employment as a District Manager to work for the Florida State Senate. It was very exciting to work in the Office of the Senate President, and my income increased quite a bit. I was able to begin tithing. I was also able to begin saving/investing money in mutual funds and paying off debt.

The positive side is that I was able to accomplish all three financial goals. The negative side is that it came with divorce. Tone' and I divorced after twenty-one years of marriage. When the divorce became final, I had become totally debt free! My mother had passed away, and the inheritance was used to pay off credit cards. I now own my own home.

I have gone from the ghetto to the Office of the Senate President. My daughter is now a medical doctor, and my son is a Master Sergeant in the United States Marines, and I own a small company. God has cared for me through all the financial struggles. His Word will not return void. Jesus said:

> *Do not worry. Then saying, What will we eat? or What will we drink? or What will we wear for clothing? . . . For your Heavenly Father knows that you need all these things. But seek first His kingdom and His righteousness, and all these things will be added to you.*
> *~Matthew 6:31-33*

Leslie DeRenzo
Email: Leslie.DeRenzo@gmail.com

MY THOUGHTS

How did this story impact you mentally?
_____
_____
_____
_____

These are the people that I will talk to if I am faced with what this author was faced with:
_____
_____
_____
_____

These are the people that I need to reach out to that may be struggling with what this author struggled with but don't have a clue that they can overcome it:
_____
_____
_____
_____

Self Motivation

I _____ understand that knowledge itself holds no power, until it is applied to our lives through our actions. I can overcome this seemingly insurmountable odd because I am Royalty from birth, making me ruler over my decisions. I will no longer live my life doubting what I am capable of overcoming.

YOU CAN CHANGE A LIFE AS WELL BY SHARING YOUR STORY........ROYALTY@MYEXCEL.COM

14
STEPPING INTO MY GREATNESS
Gerald P. Simmons, Jr.

I am sorry, Uncle Sam, for taking you up on your offer to send me back to school, and not doing the work that I was supposed to be doing. You see, my world was changed in June 2008, when I lost my job for the second time since I had gotten out of your Army in 2004. Being jobless again with a family did something to me. I knew at that point that I had to take control of my own destiny and not put it into anyone else's hands again. So when you sent me that letter, Uncle Sam, stating that I could go back to school through your program, and you would pay for it all, and give me some money every month, all I really heard was that, "You would pay me every month." I'm not saying that school is not important because it is, but an essential part of going to school is to learn and find what you want to do in life. What happens when life itself is teaching you what you need to know in order to become what you want to become in life?

    The other part of going to school is to get that degree, that wonderful piece of paper that only means you have the ability to learn whatever you put your mind to. What happens when you get out of school with your degree, and you are looking for work, but everybody is looking for experience that you don't have? What happens when you take a job that is in the same field that you have your degree in, but something totally different from what you studied? You learn the way of that company! Before I got out of the Army in December 2004, I earned my Associate Degree in Architectural Drafting, but when I went to look for work, the only job I could get was in Civil Drafting. After that job, I became a Mechanical Engineer. That was proof to me that a degree is just a piece of paper that says I have the ability to learn anything that I am taught properly and that I put my mind to. What happens when you have put your mind towards positive change, and you can teach a class that will help people be more successful in life? Do you continue to pay attention in class or do you start finally paying attention to life and help others to do the same?

Although I had the right mindset going into my online classes, it took a different turn when I had to start learning and writing about other people, disorders, statistics, and many other things that were wasting my energy and time. The only reason it was so hard for me was because I was busy trying not to become one of the negative statistics in the world. Also, by this time, I had people paying attention to what I was writing and wanting to get deeper into my mind. I had to take my destiny into my own hands, and I started studying people, and identifying what it was that kept them from bringing their greatness out for the world to see. I found out that it was the fear of the unknown, the fear of failure, and fear of not being accepted. I got sick of the same old tired mindset of "go to school so you can get a good j-o-b," and I set out to change it. Going to school to get a good job was never my goal. My goal is to get people to do what they love and want to do and not what the world forces on them. I am in the business now of motivating people to bring their greatness from within to the outside for the world to see. If college is in your path to become what you really want to be, then make sure you do what you have to do to get out of college successfully with the honors you deserve.

> *Don't ask what the world needs. Ask what makes you come alive, and go do it. Because what the world needs are people who have come alive.*—Howard Thurman

I didn't have four years to wait for that degree. You go tell my beautiful wife to hold on a little bit longer (four years) until I get that degree. I'm tired of telling her to, "Hold on a little bit longer," and I know she is getting tired of hearing it. Coming alive has not allowed me to do my school work. Every time I sit down to do some homework, I think of what I can be doing for my own business.

Many people confuse their profession with their business. To become financially secure, people need to mind their own business.—Robert Kiyosaki

I was just "minding my own business," as the great Robert Kiyosaki advised me to do. Understand that I wasn't missing school just because I was being lazy. During my absence, I had become a self-published author of the book titled, *The GPS Success Guide*; I have become a Motivational Speaker, a Certified Life Coach, and I am building my own company called Innovative Visions. Life started teaching me things that school could not teach me. Why did I go back to school, right? I will have to answer that like this, "Most people have to get a loan to go to school. Well, I had to go to school to get a loan!"

So in conclusion, I ask, "Am I wrong for trying not to be one of the negative statistics of this world and trying to build other positive statistics in this world, does that count for anything?"

GPS Success Words of Wisdom (W.o.W)   #38
Be about it rather than preach about it. In other words, walk it how you talk it! Make your life the reality you see for yourself. Define your path; don't let others do it for you. Dare to make your dreams your reality and then go beyond them according to your own visions! Guide the mind and your success will follow!

Gerald P. Simmons, Jr.
 www.GPScoach4life.com
GPS Success Will Get You There

MY THOUGHTS

How did this story impact you mentally?
_____
_____
_____
_____

These are the people that I will talk to if I am faced with what this author was faced with:
_____
_____
_____
_____

These are the people that I need to reach out to that may be struggling with what this author struggled with but don't have a clue that they can overcome it:
_____
_____
_____
_____

Self Motivation

I _____ understand that knowledge itself holds no power, until it is applied to our lives through our actions. I can overcome this seemingly insurmountable odd because I am Royalty from birth, making me ruler over my decisions. I will no longer live my life doubting what I am capable of overcoming.

YOU CAN CHANGE A LIFE AS WELL BY SHARING YOUR STORY........ROYALTY@MYEXCEL.COM

15
OVERCOMING THE STRUGGLES OF A CHILD WITH A CHRONIC ILLNESS
Dawn Desiree Banks

There were times in my life when I wanted to give up, throw my hands up, and say, "I can't do it," or "Why me?" Troubles overwhelmed me after graduating high school. I had never really gotten over my late grandparents' death. I was close to them, and I did not understand why they had departed. I was young with a hearing impairment, and my parents over-protected me. I had to witness the stages of my loved ones' illnesses and saw them slowly drift away. I still did not understand why it was all happening. I had to fight many "temptations." As a teen, I used poetry to write about any and everything that I was going through. Poetry became my therapy.

At the tender age of twenty-two, I gave birth to my first son, Keeyon, who was born on September 19, 1995. I was a new single mom. I was, by all means, "in love with my son." The nurse practitioner pulled me to the office, and told me, "Your son has the disease, called Sickle Cell Anemia, and Sickle Cell Anemia is a chronic illness." It is a disease of the blood, in which his red blood cells are sickle-shaped, making it hard for oxygen to flow through his body properly. It causes painful crises in the bones and joints of the arms, legs, back, abdomen, chest, hands, and feet. I was very afraid. I knew nothing about this disease. Trembling, I tried to leave the office in a hurry, and my baby had slid out the carrier and hit the floor. He did not even cry. I knew then that my son was "a fighter." I came home, and I cried silently.

At the age of four, I taught my son how to deal with spending time in the hospital. I assured him that the doctors and nurses were there to take care of him. I explained about the medicine that he needed to take and why it was necessary for him to take it properly. If I was not with him at the hospital, I made certain that I was on that phone with him. I knew every nurse and was knowledgeable of every shift change. I was there in time for him to eat, have any tests done, and for him to be bathed. It was my way of teaching him how to deal with being in the hospital, deal with having this illness, and knowing that I loved him. It was not easy! We battled, we fought, but God worked those miracles. I had to work and go to school. I eventually made a decision to care for him full time because his illness was unpredictable.

Subsequently, we literally lived in the hospital. At the age of six, Keeyon was given a medication called Hydroxurea. This medication was to increase his white blood count and limit the number of hospital stays. The side effects were tremendous, but we sat down, and discussed them. He and his body had been through hell and back. This medication began working wonders in our lives!

In 2001, I became pregnant with my second child, Ja'mai. Ja'mai was born with the umbilical cord wrapped around his neck, and he had stopped breathing. Ja'mai has very mild asthma, and he uses very limited medication. I balanced my time between my two children. Ja'mai was taught at the young age of six to let me know if Keeyon was in any pain. In 2006, Keeyon had a stroke. His whole left side had little feeling. It began as a pain crisis, but developed into something more. He had blood transfusions, exchanged blood transfusions, and he had to learn to walk all over again. I was mortified, stressed out, and sometimes wanted to give up. When their schedules allowed, my family was there and provided a great support system for me. Ja'mai's father was also a big help during that difficult time. Keeyon bounced back like a champ. The doctors, nurses, and the rehabilitation clinic staff was amazed at how fast he had healed and became healthy again. God was right there, continuing to work his miracles.

We all endure obstacles, trials, and tribulations. I wanted to give up! As soon as my boys were born, life changed, and I changed. I was determined to let my sons know what we were dealing with, teach them acceptance, and always knowing that they were loved. I made some mistakes along the way, but there is no such thing as a perfect person, or a perfect parent. I knew that I would never leave them. I knew that I would give them all the love I could. It was my job as mommy to show them to never ever give up on what you want to do. You may have to take a break, if you can't find your way, and that is okay, but you never ever give up. I hope my story touches someone's life. I wish for all our youth to be productive, growing with their self-esteem, accepting themselves for who they are, bringing about positive things to society, to communities, and in school. The sky is the limit!

My boys are my life, and they help keep me motivated, and give me the strength to go above and beyond. You can do anything that you want to do, as long as you believe in yourself!

I had been writing poetry since my teens and loving the works of the elegant Maya Angelou. I met briefly with Merv Mattair on a social networking site, and on that beautiful day, I learned that Merv was also blessed with a miracle. He could touch other souls with his ability to be a motivational speaker to our youth, as well as being an author. I wanted to learn more about this, so I introduced my love of writing poetry to him, and because he believed in me, he pushed me to do something with my poetry, motivated me to believe in my talents, and then introduced me to Amani Publishing, and writer Carol Griffin. On July 3, 2010, I published my first book of poetry titled, *Revelations of a Poetess*.

I was faced with struggles to stand strong during the illness of my oldest child and seemed to have succeeded. I managed to care for both of my children with the help of family and friends. Coming from many strong willed women in my family, I have strived to continue and battle all of the fights. Praise God! Keeyon is now fourteen-years-old, doing beautifully, and I am the author that I once dreamed of becoming!

Dawn Desiree Banks
Author, Poetess, Writer, Banksdesiree1@aol.com
Revelations of a Poetess, www.Amazon.com
Genesis of a Poetess, www.Silentunitypublishing.com
Facebook: http://facebook.com//dawndb

MY THOUGHTS

How did this story impact you mentally?
_____
_____
_____
_____

These are the people that I will talk to if I am faced with what this author was faced with:
_____
_____
_____
_____

These are the people that I need to reach out to that may be struggling with what this author struggled with but don't have a clue that they can overcome it:
_____
_____
_____
_____

Self Motivation

I _____ understand that knowledge itself holds no power, until it is applied to our lives through our actions. I can overcome this seemingly insurmountable odd because I am Royalty from birth, making me ruler over my decisions. I will no longer live my life doubting what I am capable of overcoming.

YOU CAN CHANGE A LIFE AS WELL BY SHARING YOUR STORY……..ROYALTY@MYEXCEL.COM

16
REAL LIFE
Brian Sanderson

It is an absolute joy to be able to share my story with you. There would be nothing worthwhile to share with you if it was all about me and not the intervening grace of God in my life. I am just one very small character in a much greater story where neither I, nor Merv, is the true author. I would like to begin in the present and work my way in reverse, hopefully, in order to reveal the redeeming and transforming qualities of God's grace. I have had the privilege of serving God as a youth pastor for the past eight years through the ministries of the church where I currently serve. I am also a graduate student at Asbury Theological Seminary where I am working on a Master Degree of Divinity which is to prepare me to be a pastor. Getting to this page of my life, however, has not been easy. I have shared this story with many young people in a variety of settings. I was scared and reluctant to share my story in the beginning. I didn't grow up in the church, and I felt that my story was very different than the stories of others that I was hearing from those inside of the church. Plus, I had returned home, where I grew up, and people outside of the church knew me, and I didn't want to come off as a hypocrite.

    I grew up with parents who loved me and did everything they could to give me more than I ever physically needed. Like all other parents, mine weren't perfect. I grew up as an only child, except for the fact that my dad was remarried and had a son who would come and stay with us on occasion. This gave my mom good reason to try and spoil me, and unfortunately, she did a good job of it. My parents, like everyone else, had habits, some were good and some were bad. Their prominent habit was their love for one another, even through the trials of life, and remained married until my mother's sudden death.

I was very well taken care of as a child. Even so, I grew up knowing that something was missing. I wanted more out of my relationship with my mother, but her addiction to alcohol robbed our family of the ability to maximize our family's relationship. It adversely affected my life.

I went through high school undisciplined, and I had trouble staying focused. I played football, basketball, and baseball during my freshman and sophomore year. I had plenty of girls, and girls became a big problem for me. I felt that I always needed a girlfriend. With my girlfriends, we never kept the relationship pure which always left me feeling jealous and overprotective. I had a need to be liked and accepted by others. I found myself trying to impress others by acting childish and foolishly which placed school work and future planning at a low priority. One day in algebra class, I was "called out and embarrassed" by a teacher, in front of the class, for talking. I stormed out and as a result, I was suspended from school. This incident occurred during the spring, and I was on the football team. We were having our spring training for the next season, and I was preparing to move up to varsity. I walked away from all of it. I walked away from my team, my school, and my friends. My family was confused and so was I. So I made the decision to transfer to a smaller Christian school in the next county. In my mind, I could start all over and become a "big fish in a small pond." Little did I know that it would be there that I would begin to fight some of the greatest battles of my life.

As I began a new school, made new friends, and joined a new football team, I remained the same person. My priorities were girls, friends, and my social status which left my grades and my true identity starved for attention. During the first semester at the new school, I developed a relationship with a girl. She and I began dating, but I had no intentions of keeping the relationship pure. So as a result, we didn't, and the relationship became sexual. One day she started getting sick and having to miss school, and this went on for a while. I was at home one afternoon watching a Florida vs. Florida State football game when she called me very upset.

She informed me that she was pregnant and that I needed to come over and bring my parents with me. As I drove to her house being followed by my parents, all that I could think of was how I had ruined both of our lives. When I arrived at her home, my biggest fear was being met at the front door by her dad and a shotgun. I felt as though I deserved it. It was hard for me to stop crying and grieving over the fact that my life was now ruined. All I could think about were the things that I wouldn't be able to do with my life now, the dreams that would be destroyed, the embarrassment, and the shame that I had caused for us. I had vowed that this would never happen to me. I had some experience with this situation since it happened to my half brother and his girlfriend several years prior, but I knew what I was doing. I resolved to help raise the baby and to support my girlfriend no matter what. Neither abortion nor adoption was ever an option for us. We could no longer attend the Christian school where we were attending. The school had rules against that sort of behavior. We both dropped out and began studying to take the General Equivalency Degree (GED) course. It was during that time that her mother asked if we would get married. I was all for the idea, but my girlfriend had some hesitation. Inside I wanted to be a man and accept responsibility for my actions and somehow make things right.

We did eventually get married which turned out to be a bad choice because we weren't really in love with each other. We were both extremely too immature, not to mention neither of us had a job or our own place to live. We both passed the GED test and began community college, and during that time our marital status became very unstable.

During the midst of these transitions, we had a beautiful baby boy. We were married for two years when we discovered that we just couldn't live together, and no matter how hard we tried, it just wouldn't work. So I moved back home with my parents and stayed in community college for another semester. I became depressed, inside I was hurting, and I lost the ability to care. I began partying, seeking happiness, and I thought drugs were the answer. As I would drink and do drugs, I found that I didn't hurt anymore, and I didn't think about my life and the numerous challenges. Unfortunately, this became a lifestyle, and it became an addiction.

As time went by, I met a girl, and we lived the party lifestyle together. Unknown to us, her parents were praying for us, and they had many others doing the same. I had always believed there was a God, but I only wanted Him to keep me safe and out of trouble. God heard their prayers, and I began to take a deep look inside of myself and became very unhappy with the person I had become. One night my mom was drunk, we got into a terrible argument, I stormed out of the house, and drove down a dirt road. I was truly "broken and sorry" for what my life had become, and I couldn't stand it any longer. It was on this dirt road where my prayer life changed dramatically. I cried out to God and begged Him to help me, forgive me, and to change me. Then and there God did something amazing! I felt God's presence in my car on that dirt road, and He gave me such peace. Over the next few weeks, God's grace began assuring me that I was forgiven of my sins. His Spirit now resided in me and was transforming me. I became so excited about what God was doing inside of me. All I could think or talk about was this new relationship I had with God and how I no longer desired to be the person I once was.

I fell in love with my girlfriend, asked her to marry me, and to share this new life with me forever. Oddly enough, she said, "Yes." I moved away to attend Bible college. We were engaged for almost two years before we were married, and she moved to be with me. During the process, I received my Associate of Arts Degree from the community college which was pending the outcome of a test. It wasn't long before my wife got pregnant, and we had our beautiful daughter. I later graduated with honors and received a Bachelor of Arts Degree in Elementary Education and Middle School Social Studies. It was during our time away at college that I realized God was calling me into full time service in His kingdom.

When you are away at college and you excel academically, the college sends the acknowledgment of your achievements to your local newspaper, and they update the community on your progress. God used that article with locals in my hometown who were members of First United Methodist Church, and they contacted me about an opening for a youth pastor position. It was never my plan to go into full-time ministry, but God wouldn't leave me alone about it, so with fear and trembling, I surrendered. After graduation, my family and I moved back to Madison and have been here since, serving the people of the church and the community. After six years of youth ministry, God's grace moved me into a season of preparation for my future ministry. I applied to and was accepted into Asbury Theological Seminary, a community called to prepare theologically educated, sanctified, spirit-filled men and women to evangelize and to spread scriptural holiness throughout the world through the love of Jesus Christ, in the power of the Holy Spirit and to the glory of God the Father. So God's grace continues, even as I write, to transform and sanctify me into the person He created me to be.

    If you're not completely sure of what your dreams are, don't worry about that right now. Your dreams will manifest at the right time, and you will passionately pursue them. Meanwhile, stay focused. Pay close attention to what you invest in, what you allow yourself to watch, to hear, to see, and say. The world has placed a large target on your back, and it spends billions of dollars a year to conform you into the world's product. Nothing will rob you of your dreams faster than conforming to the patterns of this world. Join a youth group at a church; even if you don't believe in God, there are others there who may not yet (believe Him) either. This also goes for those of you who may be too old for a youth group, but do find a church to get involved in, not to just sit in. The church is the great hope of our world. You need to surround yourself with individuals who are trying to live a moral life; those who are seeking a better way; and persons who will do good deeds in the world, and love others as themselves. Join this type of counter cultural movement. Don't be afraid of failing as you work out what it is you were created to be and to do. You are not alone, and you will not make it alone because when you are alone, the odds are insurmountable for you. God did not create you to live this life alone.

God in eternity looked down, saw me, and He saw you, foreseeing our faults, our sins, and said, "I want them to be in my family." I will do anything for them to be in my family, and I will pay for them to be in my family; and He did it with His Son's life. That is love! A crazy love! A love that is holy, unconditional, inseparable, all inclusive, atoning, deep, and eternal. That kind of love is off the radar of what we even claim to know of as love. Surrender to this love, and you'll get your focus back, and your eyes will be truly opened to see the world in a new way. You will love yourself and others as you do yourself, you will discover purpose, and you will be grafted into a new family and transformed into a new creation.

I know that our journey through life can be difficult, the times are hard, and people can be cruel. There was a time when I had no focus and thought that I didn't have a place in this world. I wanted my life to end, and I wanted a new life. God wouldn't allow me to take my own life; instead He took my life, redeemed it, and transformed me according to His kingdom purposes. I promise you that if you are hurting today that our hearts do recover, you can make it in this life. You are never alone. Find your place in the family of faith and serve the world with your gifts. You are loved!

Brian Sanderson
Youth Pastor/Master of Divinity Student:
MYF Student Ministries
First United Methodist Church
348 S.W Rutledge Street
Madison, Florida

Email: brians7901@hotmail.com
Website: brian.sanderson@asburyseminary.edu

MY THOUGHTS

How did this story impact you mentally?
_____
_____
_____
_____

These are the people that I will talk to if I am faced with what this author was faced with:
_____
_____
_____
_____

These are the people that I need to reach out to that may be struggling with what this author struggled with but don't have a clue that they can overcome it:
_____
_____
_____
_____

Self Motivation

I _____ understand that knowledge itself holds no power, until it is applied to our lives through our actions. I can overcome this seemingly insurmountable odd because I am Royalty from birth, making me ruler over my decisions. I will no longer live my life doubting what I am capable of overcoming.

YOU CAN CHANGE A LIFE AS WELL BY SHARING YOUR STORY........ROYALTY@MYEXCEL.COM

17
BE A SURVIVOR, I AM
Roshanda Denson

It all began on September 26, 1979. My mother informed me that I was an unplanned baby, and she really didn't want to have me. Yes, it's true, the enemy tried to take my life even before entering the world. My mother didn't even know me, had carried me full term, and had already made arrangements to give me to a family member. But thankfully, after seeing me for the first time, she decided to keep her only little girl.

Being raised by my mother in a house with three older and over protective brothers was hard growing up. We were poor and didn't have much. Mother worked two jobs, along with sewing to support us, and our family members also helped. She would always remind us about the rugs on the floor. She would say, "Don't step on the rugs, they are covering holes, and you all can't get sick because I can't afford to take you to the doctor."

At the age of three, I suffered a terrible breakout, losing every inch of hair on my body. People didn't know whether to call me a boy or a girl. My mother said that I went into respiratory distress, causing a reaction that could have cost my life. The reaction was caused from simply playing with a stray cat, but I survived. Later that year, I began singing in the Pentecostal church along with my family's gospel group. No one really noticed my talent at that time, and it was the tradition for all family members, including children, to sing with our family group.

At the age of nine, God began to minister to my spirit. I really didn't understand what was happening to me, but I knew I was experiencing change in my life. I always dreamed that I was standing before people singing and teaching, but I could never hear what I was singing or saying. I would remind myself daily to dream at night because living in a house not knowing where your next meal would come from, often caused me to be depressed, and sad. Dreaming at night certainly encouraged me not to give up. I never stopped dreaming, even until this very day because I am a survivor.

When I reached the age of thirteen, my older cousins and other family members had renamed me. I had been called big nose, big feet, and big lips. I was called "ugly" so much that I would answer to it when I was called. I would often avoid mirrors in the restroom, afraid of looking at what I would see. I asked my brother to take the mirror off of my dresser, break it, and place it on our front room wall to be creative. My mother liked the arrangement but never asked where the glass came from.

Many times I wanted to tell my mother, but I didn't want to take her from her rest. So I didn't, but I learned to talk to God, and I found out quickly that He would talk back to me. After hearing His voice, I began to learn the difference in wise decision making. It was the best time in my life, when I learned His voice, as it coached me to swim to the top of the pool at the Yogi Bear Park. I saw my life drifting away from me while others didn't notice me at the bottom of the pool.

The still voice said, "Come up, come up, I got you." At that very moment, I made a decision to follow that voice. It was such a blessing that I did because one hour after I almost drowned, my brother was drowning. I noticed him fighting the water, and I remember screaming for help. God sent a friend of the family to save him. Had I not obeyed that still voice, my mother would have lost two of us on the same day, but I survived.

Peer pressure was unbearable, and on a daily basis, I was continuously made fun of about my hair, my clothes, my lips, and so many other negative things. I overcame most of it with prayer and kindness. I would give humor to those that didn't care for me in an attempt for me trying to fit in. I realized later that they weren't laughing with me, but at me.

I found safety in the church and being raised in the Pentecostal church was good. We went to church four or more times a week, and I learned to give God thanks for all things, even if they weren't good.

Without church, I wouldn't have made it this far. Because I was often rejected by classmates and most family members, it left me feeling of little or no value and sometimes not knowing whether I was worth being dead or alive. I spent a lot of time and energy at the church. It was the place that I always felt that I could go when I couldn't go anywhere else. I had developed a bond with the church folk, or so I thought.

There were those who saw me working in the church and saw that I had spiritually grown in Christ in just a few short years, and it did not make them at ease. It wasn't long before I had been accused of doing something that I had not done, and it seemed to start running in a cycle. I knew it wouldn't be long before my mother would find out, and I would be disciplined for it. I was right. My mother always said that if an adult said you did it, well, you did it.

I couldn't fault my mother for trusting them because I had certainly trusted them. I knew she only wanted me to be obedient to everyone at all times. She did what most parents did in those days. I was falsely accused on many accounts, but I survived. I was raised not wearing pants, jewelry, short sleeve shirts, and opened toe shoes.

It was mandatory that on every church occasion I had to wear stockings and a covering on my head. In spite of my religious beliefs, I tried to do things that were the norm, trying to exemplify the fact that God wants us to be all we can be in whatever we do. I made the basketball team but could only play if I wore a skirt. So I did, and the pressure began rising in the church.

Some said, "Saints don't play ball," and there were others who said that I wasn't saved! Due to the uproar and the confusion in the church, my mother withdrew me from the team. I could not understand how my playing basketball was causing me "not to be a Christian." I had taken enough from everybody and everything. My spiritual growth came to a standstill, and my love for the church had grown cold. My safe place turned into a place where I no longer wanted to be. It was hard to overlook many persons who pretended to love God, but their hearts were far from Him, and so was mine.

I met someone on a day that I'll never forget. He was a few years older than me and appeared to have good Christian manners. After a few months talking on the phone, I fell in love with him. He informed me that his father was a pastor, and he was a minister. I was now fourteen, and thought I had found gold.

Secretly loving him and keeping it from my mother eventually caught up with me. I began to buy him things with "God's money," meaning my tithes and offering. I often gave him gifts to remind him how much I loved him. Three years passed, and I was sitting next to him in Kentucky Fried Chicken, on my sixteenth birthday, while we shared the kids' meal that he bought for us. During the three years, I only remember receiving a kid's meal and a used Bible case during the entire relationship.

I knew that I wasn't and had never been loved by him, but I felt I could not make it without him. Many times we went to church together, but I was never introduced to his friends or family. He would often threaten to leave me if I openly told them that we were dating. It didn't matter, or so it seemed at the time, because I just wanted to be in his presence. I was still going to church as normal, but I still had an emptiness that needed to be filled. I started to wonder if that still voice was audible again.

I longed to hear it but didn't know where to start. I had forgotten how to simply begin a conversation with God. So I went on in life, but I didn't get far. One day, my love asked me about sex. We had never spoken nor mentioned that word because we were Christians, but I became extremely aware that everyone was doing it, except me. I had hoped and prayed that he wouldn't mention it again, but lo and behold, he did. After he asked me repeatedly, I explained to him that I wanted to be married first. This caused him to go into a rage.

Not many days afterwards, he gave me an ultimatum to decide when and where we would have our first big night. I asked him, "Why can't your father marry us?" He turned and looked me straight in the face and said, "I don't want to marry you. I just want to have sex!" I knew that wasn't what I wanted to do, but I decided I would surprise him by showing up unexpectedly at his home.

Two weeks before, he had beaten me like a man, and had made me walk on a storming night for two hours.

The previous day, he had said that I wasn't pretty enough, and that it was over. But I could not allow myself to lose him. He was all I had. Lying to my mother again, faking that I was sick to stay home from church was the plan, and it worked. Never in a thousand years would I have thought that my mother knew, but that night before leaving to go to church, she said to me, "Stay away from that boy," and that went into one ear out of the other.

I quickly got dressed as she pulled off. I had bought a new outfit for the big night. After looking in the mirror, I said to myself, "I am cute! He will have to love this."

Entering his front door, I noticed that it was cracked, and I thought someone said, "Come in." As I approached the first bedroom and the dining area, I didn't see anyone. So I proceeded to the next bedroom. As I opened the door, I heard voices that I had heard before. It was the voices of my best friend and my boyfriend making out.

I fell to my knees and began to cry. I had never felt this way before. I immediately was ashamed and embarrassed that I had lied to my mother repeatedly. I had robbed and stolen God's money to give to an unworthy person. I had taken nasty name callings and excessive amounts of verbal abuse. I had given my all to him, but he had never given back to me. I began asking God to forgive me and that I was godly sorry for all the things I had done against His word. Running out to my car, the man I loved so much, grabbed me by my arm, and said, "You made me do it. If you had slept with me, this wouldn't have happened!" From out of nowhere, I got the strength and the power to tell him, "It's over!"

Although he tried on many attempts to get back with me, I went back to my first love. He didn't have a chance of messing that up again, and I refused to allow him to. It was so good to hear that still voice again. God reminded me of how he kept me all those years, just to form and shape me into a useful vessel. I was poor, teased, falsely accused, lied on, misunderstood, forsaken, picked out to be picked on, failing health, survived a car wreck that caused permanent nerve damage to the lower part of my body, and a broken tailbone, but I walked out, and I rose above it all. Through my suffering, my hardships, and my safe return to Him, God rewarded me with a godly, respectful, and supportive man who loves everything about me and more. I am proud to announce that my husband of eleven years claimed my virginity.

At the age of thirty-one, I am a successful prison nurse, a musician, songwriter, youth minister, and a new gospel recording artist. To you, who have read my story, please remember that dreams do come true, and always know God wants to hear from you. Be a survivor, I am!

Roshanda Denson
Email: densonroshanda@yahoo.com

MY THOUGHTS

How did this story impact you mentally?
_____
_____
_____
_____

These are the people that I will talk to if I am faced with what this author was faced with:
_____
_____
_____
_____

These are the people that I need to reach out to that may be struggling with what this author struggled with but don't have a clue that they can overcome it:
_____
_____
_____
_____

Self Motivation

I _____ understand that knowledge itself holds no power, until it is applied to our lives through our actions. I can overcome this seemingly insurmountable odd because I am Royalty from birth, making me ruler over my decisions. I will no longer live my life doubting what I am capable of overcoming.

YOU CAN CHANGE A LIFE AS WELL BY SHARING YOUR STORY……..ROYALTY@MYEXCEL.COM

18
A QUEST FOR MANHOOD
David Dukes

Throughout the continent of Africa, several tribes practice initiations: Rites of passage. I will focus on the rite from boyhood to manhood. It has to do with real men, not male human beings. I am talking about men of character, men with integrity, real fathers, real husbands, and real keepers of the flame/light, and never allowing it to cease to burn and illuminate our path. We must be on the job in season and out of season.

I was born in Madison, Florida. My daddy abandoned us when I was young. I began asking myself, "How am I supposed to become a real man when I do not have anyone to teach me how this transition is supposed to take place?" I wondered about the transition from boyhood to young man, from young man to real man.

There was/is no road map to follow. It must be taught by real men to young men. I heard from the street what a real man was about having lots of sex with anyone who would allow it, and if he did not, he boasted that he was. Making a baby was not a big deal because it was always her fault. He had to have big muscles, a vulgar mouth, consume a lot of alcohol, beat up his wife/girlfriend to show who was in charge, the size of a certain part of his physical anatomy had to be big, and he always had to talk about trivial insignificant nonsense. That is what I heard from the streets about what a real man was supposed to be.

I asked, "Will I ever become a real man?" The things I heard from the streets did not come close to any of the criterion of my definition of a real man. I walked the dirt roads seeking real men who I could pattern myself after. I found very few who measured up to the standards I had set for myself. I was low-rated and talked about because of these standards.

At the age of fifteen, I accepted Jesus Christ as my personal savior. It was very important to me to be a real Christian man and not just a religious man or a religious churchgoer. The life that I lived had to reflect the moral standards that had been laid down by Jesus Christ. It must be practiced daily and not only at eleven o'clock on Sunday morning. It did not affect me when males fell from grace from the basketball court, the golf course, the football field, the wrestling ring, the congress, the pulpit, or any other place, or position because I did not worship them in the first place.

During the spring/summer months of the year, the mockingbirds, the State bird of Florida, were seen seeking and gathering small twigs, and other items, to make a nest/house for their future family. After a while, a dark mass, their nest, appeared in a certain part of the tree. As time passed, a bird was sitting on the eggs all the time and soon the eggs hatched. One could not know there was a nest in a certain tree until you walked under or near the tree. A person could find themselves being attacked by the birds. The mockingbird would attack people, cats, dogs, snakes, or any other creatures that they felt was a threat to their young. Each day, the mother and father bird were out seeking food for their young. When the young birds became old enough, they were taught how to fly and hunt.

I could never understand why a judge has to order a male human being to take care of his children. The judge did not order the male human being to make a baby. Writing a child support check never fulfills all the needs of a child. I have met too many young male human beings who could learn a serious lesson from the mockingbirds.

Do not go out making babies without having the resources or the commitment to take care of them; no education, no job, no home to raise them, nor have sense enough to raise the offspring. Others in the community stigmatized a child by calling it illegitimate. The old folks used to say, "Don't put the cart before the horse."

I've met too many young male human beings who thought making babies made them men. We have a serious problem because too many of our young boys are masquerading as men.

My foundation to manhood was becoming more powerful. You cannot shake me now. It has made me free. I am able to stand firm on what I believe, my principles and moral standards without any fear of losing a job, manmade prestige, or my life. I was told to learn to compromise. There are things I will compromise, but some I will not consider because without them, I will be an empty shell. I will not be an empty shell for anyone. I cannot be what ten people want me to be—I've got to be me! My serious efforts of self-control have paid off. I do not have to prove anything to anyone based on their standards for me. I do not live my life by standards that others have set for me.

Brothers, we must resist all temptations. I know it is not easy at times, but we must carry the torch of real manhood in season and out of season. We must teach our young brothers by words, deeds, and actions. Lip service is no longer an option. We must allow our little light to shine at all times.

A real man is measured by the content of his character and the standards of his mind, not by the nonsense I heard from the streets. I am still at peace with myself because I did not give in to the nonsense.

Am I my brother's keeper? Yes, I am my brother's keeper. I do not participate in drive-by shootings. Yes, I am my brother's keeper. I do not steal from my brothers, or anyone else. I do not buy stolen goods from my brothers. I do not sell crack cocaine to my brothers. I do not use crack cocaine. I do not neglect my family or my other responsibilities. Yes, I am my brother's keeper. I do not call my brothers nigger. I do not wear my pants falling off of my rear end. Yes, I am my brother's keeper. I do not participate in illegal and criminal activities. Yes, I have served time in jail. It was an honor to go to jail for leading the Civil Rights War of the 1960's in Madison County, Florida.

Madison taught me hate. I decided to try love. Madison taught me violence. I decided to try non-violence. Madison taught me hypocrisy. I decided to be real and not allow anyone to play games with me. Madison taught me injustice. I decided to stand for justice. Madison taught me fear. I decided not to fear any man or anything. I was forced to leave Madison in 1965. I could no longer tolerate the daily insults, the arrests, the harassments, and the threats by hateful individuals. I returned in 1993 to give back to my community.

My advice to my young kings and queens: Plant your feet, your entire being, on a solid foundation. Know who you are. Do not allow anyone to define who you are. Set your principles and moral standards in place, and do not allow anyone to cause you to waiver or tamper with them. Do not go along in order to get along. Let us know who you are by the life you live! Integrity is the key!

David Dukes
Author, Human Rights Advocate, Youth Advocate, and African-American History Speaker

Author of *I Have Never Lived in America* and *A Journey Back Home: The Story of the Johnson-Brinson Project & Break Away*. Available at: www.authorhouse.com; www.amazon.com; www.bn.com; www.borders.com; and ddukes45@hotmail.com

MY THOUGHTS

How did this story impact you mentally?
_____
_____
_____
_____

These are the people that I will talk to if I am faced with what this author was faced with:
_____
_____
_____
_____

These are the people that I need to reach out to that may be struggling with what this author struggled with but don't have a clue that they can overcome it:
_____
_____
_____
_____

Self Motivation

I _____ understand that knowledge itself holds no power, until it is applied to our lives through our actions. I can overcome this seemingly insurmountable odd because I am Royalty from birth, making me ruler over my decisions. I will no longer live my life doubting what I am capable of overcoming.

YOU CAN CHANGE A LIFE AS WELL BY SHARING YOUR STORY........ROYALTY@MYEXCEL.COM

19
From Stuttering to Motivational Speaking
Marvin "Merv" Mattair

As a young man, I was made aware of a speech impediment that caused me to be unable to engage in a normal conversation with friends and family. Speech Therapists identified the problem as stuttering, and yes, I had it bad. I remember at one point in my life, I was able to complete full sentences in a timely manner without stumbling over my words, but once I started to hang around guys who struggled verbally, I soon began to struggle in the same area. At the age of fifteen, I can remember being in the presence of family members during a family gathering and afraid to join the conversations. Completing a full sentence, without pausing or stumbling over my words, was seemingly impossible. When I did jump into the conversations, I would only embarrass myself to the point that I wanted to run and hide. Although some friends and family did not want to actually laugh in my face, I could see the smirk on their faces when I struggled to say a simple sentence. But as you know, some friends and family would burst out in laughter.

A lot of my fights and outbursts as a young man came from my anger and aggravation. It was a challenge not being able to do something as simple as holding a casual conversation to explain myself with someone older or even younger. The line was drawn, when one day at the age of twenty, I was being introduced to this pastor, and when I shook the guy's hand, he simply looked me into my eyes and asked, "How are you doing young man?" I could not get one word out of my mouth. No, I was not nervous, my words just refused to come out, and I had to stand there and watch this man watching me, hoping his question would be answered, but it did not happen. The man just patted me on the shoulder, and walked away with a smirk on his face. I wanted to wake up out of that dream, but the reality was, I was not sleeping.

I was tired and I knew that there had to be a better way, so I searched for my answer in the Bible. As I read different Scriptures, I started to notice that talking too much can be very harmful to us, and utilizing silence is powerful, so guess what I started doing? I now had something to hide behind to keep my impediment from being exposed, so I started to promote the saying, "There is power in silence." Although this is a true statement, I was using it for protection of possible embarrassment. I was quick to send people to Scriptures to back that up, but ultimately, I was protecting Merv.

I knew that I could not hide much longer, and I would have to do something to strengthen my speech impediment because I was getting a strong passion for working with young people, writing books, and public speaking. I started to pray about my situation, but the more I prayed, the more guys I would come into contact with whom had the same challenge with regard to speaking with ease. So I felt like I was doomed for life. I remember sitting down with the family watching a family recording of an event that had been hosted earlier, and as the tape progressed, I remember talking on the tape, and I could not understand what I was saying because I could not complete a sentence. Man that was painful to watch and hear, so I figured that in order to improve this problem, I was going to have to listen to myself again and again to find out what I was doing wrong.

Instead of looking at that tape again, I went out and bought a small tape recorder, recorded myself talking, and then played it back a number of times. As I did that a few times, I began to realize that I did not sound confident when I spoke, and I was not thinking of the words before I said them. I went a step further by asking Denise, my girlfriend (now my wife) to help me, by holding me accountable when I did not take my time to form my words. And boy, did she do her job well! I did not like being called out like that, but I asked for it, and I knew that I needed it in order to overcome that which was holding me back from fulfilling my purpose. Through the use of the little cheap tape recorder, I started to get better and better because I encouraged myself to be confident when I spoke, and I formed the words in my mind before they came out of my mouth.

I continued to do it daily for the next few months until I was able to see results through my daily conversations. I overcame a seemingly insurmountable odd in my life because I wanted more, and I knew that nothing could hold me down except me. Faith and works, confidence, self motivation, and a cheap tape recorder skyrocketed me *from stuttering to motivational speaking*. I delivered my first speech in 2004 at the Fine Arts Auditorium at North Florida Community College to over 500 adults and children. Serving as the African-American Student Union President, I was able to successfully implement what I had worked so hard to overcome. Since that time, I have spoken to thousands of youth and adults at several schools and programs as well as writing my first ever published book titled, *Word To My Kings & Queens: Achieving A Renewed & Improved Mind*.

I am blessed to say that I overcame a seemingly insurmountable odd in my life, and you can too. I noticed a change in my actions, once defeating the impediment because I started to apply for positions at my previous job that would allow me to be in positions to speak out to and for other people. My increased level of confidence landed me in a program director's role in a corporate setting. If there is something in your life that's holding you back from your greatness, don't be afraid to ask for help, be willing to go the extra mile for yourself, and be confident that anything that you put your mind to will be overcome. Don't ever feel that you are stuck in a situation just because the odds seem to be against you. To this day, I may stumble from time to time, but that's only to remind me to not forget where I've come from. You have a mind to think your way out of any situation, as long as you have the desire and confidence to do so. YOU ARE ROYALTY—Peace & Ubuntu, Merv

Marvin Terrell Mattair, BKA Merv
Author, Motivational Speaker, Youth Advocate, and Contractor

Email: royalty@myexcel.com

Website: www.kingsqueens.org

MY THOUGHTS

How did this story impact you mentally?
_____
_____
_____
_____

These are the people that I will talk to if I am faced with what this author was faced with:
_____
_____
_____
_____

These are the people that I need to reach out to that may be struggling with what this author struggled with but don't have a clue that they can overcome it:
_____
_____
_____
_____

Self Motivation

I _____ understand that knowledge itself holds no power, until it is applied to our lives through our actions. I can overcome this seemingly insurmountable odd because I am Royalty from birth, making me ruler over my decisions. I will no longer live my life doubting what I am capable of overcoming.

NOT THIS ONE
A Rally of All Parents

To my dear parents of this world, I am here to do one thing and one thing only, and that is to **Rally the Troops!** As parents, we are in a different kind of war that requires us to get off the back line, and serve on the front line. In this day and age, we can no longer do a little and expect a lot. Being a parent has never been easy, but it has never been this hard. Each year brings about new challenges for our youth that sometimes suck them in, and then spit them out down the wrong path, making it harder for them to make it back to the path that they were once on. No longer can we allow this to happen to our precious children, without attempting to do something about it in a proactive way. *The school teachers, faculty, and staff are trying, but they can't do it by themselves; the government is trying, but they can't do it by themselves; pastors can pray all day, but they can't do it on their actions and faith alone; and youth organizations are trying around the clock, but they can't do it by themselves either.*

Parents, it's going to require that we, individually and collectively, do our parts; we must do this daily, without wavering, standing up, and dealing with the forces that come to destroy the minds of our kids. I am tired of hearing in the media, sitting in meetings and hearing conversations about parents who are not doing enough for their children. Because I am a parent, I feel that I share some of the blame. When we begin to understand the *power of the 4P's* (in this order), **Parents-Pastors-Principles-Politicians**, we will understand that all of them should be operating in the best interest of our kids; and for the most part, I feel assured that they are. It's only when we don't lead them, and don't do our part, that our youth fall through the cracks, and it appears as though they are not doing their part, when in reality, they can't fully succeed when we slack in our duties. Well, parents, enough is enough! So let's "strap up mentally," and do our part through prayer, fasting, faith, confidence, sacrifice, dedication, and endurance.

There is no such thing as the back line or the second line anymore; there is only one line, and it's the front line. Sometimes being on the front line, we are going to get hit with stuff that may knock us down. But we must get up immediately, realizing that if we stay down too long, we may fall asleep, and while we are snoring (making a lot of noise with no action behind it), and "counting sheep," our youth are being heavily tempted by musical lyrics, rated-X conversations, and visual images that the world offers them.

While we count sheep, our youth are getting pregnant and making babies. *While we count sheep*, out youth are disrupting school functions, and receiving failing grades, causing great teachers to throw in the towel; and causing new teachers to develop bad habits in order to gain control. *While we count sheep*, our youth are being molested by family members and friends. *While we count sheep*, our youth are dodging bullets, fighting and selling drugs in the streets; and *while we count sheep*, our youth are being bound down in jails, prisons, and juvenile programs, and being stripped of their lives and liberty.

So, it's time to **get up** for some, **wake up** for others, and **keep going strong** for the rest. The enemy wants and needs us out of the way, in order to get to our kids, but **I don't think so!** We say to the enemy, this is my child and although you have a great past record of destroying the minds of our youth, and tossing obstacles in the way of parents that cause us to struggle, and lose interest in the future of our kids, and fall asleep, we now stand on the front line as a supportive, concerned, and wide awaken parent with our child (children) behind us to say to you, "Not This One."

We say to the negative forces of drugs and drug dealers, "Not This One." We say to the negative forces of slick talking boys and perverted men who come to misuse and abuse our daughters, "Not This One." We say to the negative forces through older women who come seeking youthful pleasures from our sons, "Not This One." We say to the negative forces of the media that comes to replace the values that we have placed inside of our kids with lies, violence, hobby sex, greed, and hatred, "Not This One." We say to the negative forces of sexually transmitted diseases, "Not This One." We say to the negative forces of poverty, "Not This One." We say to the negative forces of prisons and juvenile facilities, "Not This One." We say to the negative forces of bullying or being bullied, "Not This One," and we say to the negative forces of racial teachings and injustice, "Not This One."

Will we occasionally fall on this journey, causing certain things to come upon our children? Yes, but that's not always our fault because sometimes circumstances are out of our control. There are times when we fall because we are only human, and our youth definitely have minds of their own. It's only when we don't get involved, or refuse to get up, and make the best of any given situation that it becomes our fault.

I'm calling ALL: single mothers, single fathers, absent fathers, wives, husbands, grandparents, guardians, god-parents, mentors, and step-parents to stand in the gap, at least try, and say with firmness, boldness, and confidence, "Not this one!" If we have several kids, we must stand for them individually because each child has his/her own negative forces pulling at them daily. It will not be easy, and to be honest, nobody ever said that it would be. We are going hard, so that one day our kids can stand on their own, when we are not around, and be able to say to the enemy, "Not this one, Homey."

Get ready world! The troops have been rallied, and we are taking our kids back! If you don't mind making it known to the world that you pledge to stand on the front line for the empowerment of our youth, let it show through your actions first, then if you desire to, place your name on the Not This One Roster at: www.kingsqueens.org .

YOU SAVED ME
Marvin "Merv" Mattair

This extended dedication is written in honor of Mr. HB, former employee of the Madison County Memorial Hospital in Madison, Florida. This man's unselfish actions preserved the physical structure of my family.

On August 8, 2008, my wife and I were blessed with a three-pound premature son by the name of TJ. Due to his premature status, he had to stay in the hospital for several weeks. We travelled back and forth to Tallahassee to sit with him and to give him his daily baths. Once he reached the required weight and was able to do a few things on his own, we were able to bring him home. We had the football decorations on the wall in his room, the football rug, the little baby crib ready, and so much more. After weeks of traveling back and forth, we were relieved to finally get him home.

Five days after our little prince came home, little did we know that we were about to experience a life changing event. On September 11, 2008, around midnight, while my family was resting, I was up *writing my thoughts*. As I approached my little son during one of the many night checks, I noticed a white substance coming out of his nose and a discoloration of his lips, making it obvious that he had not been breathing since my last check from two to three minutes ago. I began to call out his name while pushing on his little left arm, but to no avail. "No, God, No!" I screamed over and over as I ran through the house with him in my arms to find my wife.

Once I got to her, she jumped out the bed and I screamed, "Baby, he's not breathing!" As a mommy, I was hoping that she could fix the problem, but as she attempted to perform cardiopulmonary resuscitation (CPR), it was obvious that our little son was gone. I ran outside as if I were in a dream and ignited the vehicle. By the time I made it back to the front door, my wife met me with our little son wrapped in a blanket, and all I could see was one of his little legs dangling from the short side of the linen. With my daughter in the backseat and my son in my lap, I accidentally left my wife behind. I raced down Highway 90 in search of the Madison County Hospital while continually pumping his little chest and breathing into his mouth the best I could.

Once we reached our destination, we stormed into the emergency room entrance, and I cried out for anyone to, "Please save my son!" Immediately, a woman in the waiting room burst out in a loud prayer, and a white male nurse came and removed TJ from my arms, and took him into another room. While they performed an intense CPR session on his tiny body, I got in a corner without any fear of embarrassment, and I prayed and cried out to God. After about a minute of silence from that room, I heard my little man cry, and that was "a defining moment in my life." While holding TJ in my arms inside of the operating room, together with my wife, mom, dad and several other supporters, my mom whispered to me, "Merv, you know that guy that just saved TJ's life, when I walked outside just now, I noticed him crying." I could not picture this guy because I had not really looked at him.

The long trip in the ambulance back to Tallahassee, with TJ in my arms, holding a breathing mask over his face, gave me a major reality check. Two days later, when I arrived back from the Tallahassee hospital, I found this guy, and I hugged him as if I had known him my entire life. I could only thank God for Mr. HB because his timely actions saved my family a lot of grief. As a "thank you," we decided to give Mr. HB the only copy of our first book that displayed TJ's little footprints at birth inside of it. That made his night!

We teach our kids to respect and love everyone, no matter their race, religion, or social status because as long as we are on this earth, we never know who we will be depending on, or who will lend us a helping hand at critical moments in our lives. Everybody in the earth serves purpose, and we must learn to acknowledge that fact. So rest in peace, Mr. HB . . .

Acknowledgements

I acknowledge that most people desire to share their stories with the world but don't have a venue. So if you would like to change a life by adding your story to our next book, don't hesitate to contact us at: Royalty@myexcel.com

    I would, first of all, like to thank God for blessing and keeping me while I travel through this life. The first person that I give thanks to is my wife and queen, Denise, because if it were not for you being the woman that you are, I know that I would not be complete, so thank you, and I love you so very much. To my kids, Lyric and TJ, Daddy loves you both so much, and I only want the best for you. I pray for you and encourage you to protect your minds at all cost, and do not allow this world to dictate your level of love for each other and your fellowman. To my Dad and Mom, Curtis and Shirley Mattair, I thank you both for being the unconditionally loving parents that you are and have always been. As I look back over my life, I can clearly see that *I am who I am because of whom my Father was*. The stability in my home, the love for my kids, the hustling attitude, the physical endurance during struggling times, the respect for others, and the hunger for physical fitness is a reflection of your presence Dad, so thanks for not walking out on me. To all of my siblings: Curtis Mattair Jr., Kelvin Mattair, Elshauntey Mattair, Rosaline Mattair, and Shantel Wise, thank you for helping to shape the canvass of my life. Brother and sister-in-laws: R.I.P Jody Joseph, Choya Wise, Tosheba Joseph, Lynduell Mattair, Elayne Weatherspoon, and Jimmy Weatherspoon, we are blessed that each of you chose to be a part of our family or allowed me to be a part of yours. To the 2010-2011 Boyz to Kings family, I thank you guys for trying your best to become mature leaders on this earth, and for every supportive BTK parent for solidifying the fact that *parents will get involved*. I am proud and a big congratulation to the little 2010 eight to ten year-old Lions for bringing home the football trophy with a 10-0 record and a history making moment for the league, I want all of you guys to know that we work/worked you hard for you to be successful in (not just football or the BTK Family), but in this walk of life. We need you to be great fathers, leaders, husbands, etc., so go hard at everything positive that you set your mind to and never doubt who or what you can become or accomplish. Lions' parents, thank you for supporting the league with your time and efforts. Your cheering at games, your attendance at practices, and the painting of your vehicles for away games will always be in the minds of those youth, and they will carry that on to give to their kids. Thanks to Morningstar Missionary Baptist Church (Pastor Oliver Bradley) for allowing us to practice the past five years on your property. Thanks for my awesome and supportive assistant coaches, Coach Curtis (Pops), Coach Dustin, Coach Jake, Coach Kendrick, and Coach Chris. To my mother and father-in-laws: Shirley Souter, Carlton Souter, and Clenon Joseph, Sr., my nieces and nephews, and to all of my family members in Gainesville, Lake Butler, Orlando, Tallahassee, Live Oak, Madison, Florida, Canada (Tim Tuxworth & Family), Australia (Gail Tuxworth & family), and Alabama, I would like to spread a word of love to all of you.

    I give thanks to Mrs. Edna Haynes-Turner for editing this book to the best of her ability. Mrs. Edna, you have really demonstrated the meaning of the word support because you walk it first then talk about the outcome later. To all of the phenomenal and powerful women: Denise, Devona, Edna, Evelyn, and Tosheba, who worked behind the scenes that allowed me to pull off my first ever *Youth Explosion* on May 8, 2010. To all of the fathers who are trying to do the best they can at being ideal fathers and role models, I say *keep persevering, even though the majority of the publicity is focused on the negative, rather than the numerous fathers who are positively impacting the lives of their children*. I am asking each of you reading this, to take out the time and acknowledge the man who is trying to be the best father that he can. To all the past recipients of the, "My Small Town Hero Award," please continue to let your light shine because that award is proof that you were being watched and appreciated. To Mr. David Dukes, for being a supportive elder in my life for the past three years. When I read this Civil Rights Leader's books and biography, it really touched me because he did so much for the betterment of oppressed people. He still resides on this earth, yet he's hardly ever recognized for his struggles and contributions. I read the hundreds of letters from youth telling you thanks for taking out the time to make them better citizens without having the proper funds to operate. I saw the unedited videos of youth interacting at your facility for long periods of time without hearing them say one negative word. I saw the videos of you standing in front of community leaders asking for a little support and evidently not receiving your desired amount and I have heard you speak with truth and so much passion that it was perceived as anger by the ones who wanted to hide behind a lie and not deal with the truth of how things really were. During the Civil Rights Era, you were committed, and a force to be reckoned with, and positively impacted the lives of all African-Americans. I will not wait until God calls you home before I choose to recognize you, for all that you have given, sacrificed, and the change you helped to create locally, statewide, and nationally. So, all readers please add Mr. David Dukes to your list of living Civil Rights Leaders for documentaries, book signings, and speaking engagements. To Jamarien Purcell Moore, keep up the great work for Christ with your singing and your daily walk and if anyone have not heard this young man sing, you're missing out on a blessing. To Ervin Haynes, I must say that I am proud of you for becoming the family man that you have become and how strong you were after losing your dad. Stay strong my brother and don't give up because I love you, and I need you to be successful. To Wayne Frazier, I say thanks for helping me start the BTK family because your support was really needed and greatly appreciated. You have a beautiful family and a supportive wife, so stay strong mentally and let nothing or no one make you think differently (I Love you Bro.). To "My Best Man," David Williams AKA Gator, you have the heart of Christ my brother, and I will always think highly of you. I pray that your marriage be successful and full of joy. To Charlie Fulmer

Sr., you are a true example of a king and I want to continue to learn from you sir, because you not only talk about loving your wife and spending quality time with your kids, you demonstrate it daily through your walk. To Tharron Robinson, I encourage you to keep being the best Deacon, husband, and father that you can because your success is someone else's success. You will be surprised at the men who base what they can do off of what you're doing, so don't grow weary brother because your good works are not in vain. To Uncle Horace Cherry, Sr., I must say that men like you don't come by often and that a lot of your attributes I try to gain through watching you. To Savetria Robinson-Williams, please continue to practice your faith in the building of your business and it will be a success. If you are having a banquet, a wedding, or if you may need planning for a party, and you want your fantasies to become a reality, Mrs. Sevetria wants you to contact: Exquisite Affairs Event Planning@ ssr05@embarqmail.com.

      To Pastor Marcus Hawkins & Mrs. Hawkins, being in your twenties and thirties, the both of you are really making an impact on the lives of a lot of people with your walking of God's Word, not just the preaching of it, so I encourage you to not let your mistakes, your lack of, your trials or your haters steal your joy. If you have not heard this young man bring the Word, then I encourage you to stop by Shiloh Missionary Baptist Church the next chance that you get or the next time that you're passing through the City of Madison, Florida. A big thanks to the Madison County Fast Pitch Softball Coaches, Rusty Smith, Johnny, Rick, Steve, and Todd, for protecting, respecting, and teaching my daughter, Lyric, about the sport. You guys proved that others can impact the lives of our children as well, but we have to get the youth involved and keep them engaged. When I see her playing at the high school level currently, I think back to when she was just six years of age and how she stuck with it through you guys giving of your time and pushing her as well as involving me in the practices, etc. Thanks guys. To the 2006-2008 Jefferson House Staff and my assistant supervisor, Angela Turner Rooks, I want to say that I love you all, and I thank you for giving me the opportunity to prove what the power of love can do, even for a cabin full of twelve to nineteen year-old male juvenile delinquents. We learned together that when the head don't show love, don't give recognition, don't hold accountable, don't give respect, or refuse to get involved with the staff first and the clients second, that chaos arises. We did it because you all did not work for me, you worked with me, so keep blessing those youth and insure that your environment is full of love and not hate. To Sue Singleton and Mike Blue, working with youth was only a vision at one point in my life, but you two made it a reality by giving me a chance, teaching me, holding me accountable, and allowing me to dream, so I will forever remember you. To Steven and Donna Cuccinella, I thank you for giving me the opportunity to be a part of your rock band (St. Stephens). To Mr. Pat Lightcap and Mrs. Lightcap, I really thank you two for welcoming my family into your home at any giving time and for trying your best to get my efforts recognized by submitting information to news stations, etc. To Krystal Green, for taking care of our son, TJ, during his premature months as his personal baby sitter (Thank you). To Mt. Zion AME Church of Cherry Lake, Florida, Shiloh Missionary Baptist Church (Pastor Marcus Hawkins) of Madison Florida, Bethlehem Missionary Baptist Church of Madison, Florida. (Pastor Colson), Superintendant Lou Miller, and the Madison County School District, Mr. Oliver Bradley for the radio time, Live the Life Ministries of Tallahassee, Florida, Mrs. Killings, Monticello Correctional Facility, and many more for supporting the writing ministry of my first book by purchasing a copy or spreading the word. Your support really gave me a major boost of motivation, and I am forever grateful. It is easy to act like we don't see someone trying to follow their dreams than it is to support them, so you and several more decided to give me that support therefore I say thank you.

I love you all.

Marvin "Merv" Mattair

About the Visionary

Mr. Merv is a thirty-two-year-old husband, father to a fourteen-year-old queen, and a two-year-old future king. This is his second release following his first book titled, *Word to My Kings & Queens: Achieving a Renewed & Improved Mind*. In that book, he gave a lot of recognition to his father for taking care of his responsibilities.

He also reached out to all youth and adults with the message that, "We cannot move forward until we know who we are, and then decide to do things differently through the acquiring of a renewed and improved mind."

Mr. Merv believes strongly in the walking of the Word, more so than the preaching of it. One of his desires is to continue being a faithful husband to his queen and a supportive father to his kids.

Given the fact that temptations are stronger now than ever; he created a network for men who support and help each other to be the ideal man for their children, wives, and communities. Mr. Merv makes it clear that falling unnecessarily and losing our families is no longer an option because ultimately, our kids will suffer.

He admits that he needs this network of brothers because he is only human himself and not being open about individual struggles only lead to failure. If you are a male, seventeen or older, feel free to join at www.menofroyalty.ning.com.

He is the Visionary of R.O.Y.A.L.T.Y. N/O, Inc. where motivational speaking, youth empowerment explosions, book writing, book signings, and contracting are at its finest. Spreading love, motivating youth, supporting families, renewing minds, and role modeling are only a few of Merv's passions that keep him going daily.

For more information about this young powerful Visionary, check out his website at: www.kingsqueens.org, email him at: royalty@myexcel.com, or find him on www.facebook.com .

Supporting another individual's dream is genuine when we do it even before our own dream becomes a full reality. ~

Marvin "Merv" Mattair

www.ingramcontent.com/pod-product-compliance
Lightning Source LLC
Chambersburg PA
CBHW031257290426
44109CB00012B/627